CW01467218

THREE PERSPECTIVES OF ANTHROPOSOPHY

CULTURAL PHENOMENA FROM THE POINT OF VIEW OF SPIRITUAL SCIENCE

THREE PERSPECTIVES OF ANTHROPOSOPHY

CULTURAL PHENOMENA FROM THE POINT OF VIEW OF SPIRITUAL SCIENCE

Twelve lectures held in Dornach between
5 May and 23 September 1923

TRANSLATED BY ELIZABETH MARSHALL

INTRODUCTION BY ELIZABETH MARSHALL

RUDOLF STEINER

RUDOLF STEINER PRESS

CW 225

Rudolf Steiner Press
Hillside House, The Square
Forest Row, RH18 5ES

www.rudolfsteinerpress.com

Published by Rudolf Steiner Press 2021

Originally published in German under the title *Drei Perspektiven der Anthroposophie. Kulturphänomene, geisteswissenschaftlich betrachtet* (volume 225 in the Rudolf Steiner Gesamtausgabe or Collected Works) by Rudolf Steiner Verlag, Dornach. Based on shorthand notes that were not reviewed or revised by the speaker. This authorized translation is based on the second German edition (1990) that was edited by Hella Wiesberger und Ruth Moering

Published by permission of the Rudolf Steiner Nachlassverwaltung, Dornach

© Rudolf Steiner Nachlassverwaltung, Dornach, Rudolf Steiner Verlag 1990

This translation © Rudolf Steiner Press 2021

All rights reserved. No part of this publication may be reproduced, stored in a retrieval system, or transmitted, in any form or by any means, electronic, mechanical, photocopying or otherwise, without the prior permission of the publishers

A catalogue record for this book is available from the British Library

ISBN 978 1 85584 587 9

Cover by Andrew Morgan
Typeset by Symbiosys Technologies, Vishakapatnam, India
Printed and bound by 4Edge Ltd., Essex

CONTENTS

spiritual in culture. How to bring the spiritual back into culture? Anthroposophy on Schweitzer's cultural criticism.

Pages 28-44

DORNACH, 6 JULY 1923
A study of the century from 1823 to 1923

Literary characteristics of George Sand and the scientific study of history. Goethe's *Wilhelm Meister* compared to Sand's novel, *The Journeyman Joiner*. Goethe writes in a cosmopolitan manner, Sand national, political. French artisan associations—'Loups Devorants' and 'Gavots'. Differences between these groups. Devorants and human astrality; Gavots and the human 'I'. The tendency of artisans towards the spiritual. Emulation of spiritual fellowships in Masonic secret societies. Differences in the colour of blood in various climate zones. Human beings in relation to the spiritual impulses active in various geographic areas. A catechism for wandering carpenters in France. A study of history from the perspective of spiritual science.

Pages 45-56

DORNACH, 7 JULY 1923
Community building in Central Europe

Different concepts of intellectualism have existed since the fifteenth century. Life and work in the West in contrast to the free spirituality in Central Europe. Individual artisans with a thirst for knowledge of alchemy and astrology. Education in Western and Central Europe. Goethe's human wisdom in *Wilhelm Meister*. Female personalities as 'seers' at the beginning of the nineteenth century. Contribution of newspapers to the destruction of spiritual life. Effectiveness of astrology on the nerve-sense system. Effectiveness of alchemy on the metabolic system. Balance of both systems in Paracelsus and Faust. Human education in Central and Western Europe. The tolerance of the East seen in the letters of Dostoevsky on Switzerland and Germany. On the necessity, from a national point of view, of becoming a citizen of the earth. History and geography need a spiritual metamorphosis.

Pages 57-68

DORNACH, 8 JULY 1923
European culture and its relationship to the Latin language
Greek and Roman mysteries

The logic of reason encourages materialism. Eastern Europe and Greek consciousness. Western and Central Europe and Latin education. The Latin

Dornach, 23 September 1923

Jakob Boehme, Paracelsus, Swedenborg

Intellectual conceptualizing and dreaming with sensations and feelings. Somnambulants such as Boehme and Swedenborg and the influence of the moon. Great teachers of earth wisdom as present-day moon beings. On reproductive life on earth. The interior of the moon and what is reflected back from it. Earthiness and moon power in the human etheric body. Hostility of somnambulants towards the spirit in pre-earthly existence. Somnambulants and spiritual experience on earth. The ability of Boehme and of Swedenborg to perceive transitional states. Knowledge of the Druids in connection with light and shadow. Atavism in Boehme and Paracelsus. Musical compositions at the end of the nineteenth century compared to the statements of Boehme. Swedenborg's power of Saturn. Tasks of such people as Swedenborg in the post-earthly world. Supersensible beings who dwell in humans.

INTRODUCTION

T HIS volume of the Collected Works of Rudolf Steiner consists of 12 lectures given over the summer of 1923 from 5 May to 23 September. It was a portentous year at the very beginning of which stands the tragedy of the fire which burned down the first Goetheanum in Dornach. At the end stands the Christmas Conference and the re-founding of the Anthroposophical Society with the Foundation Stone meditation at its heart. In the intervening year Steiner came to regard the Society and most of its members as incapable of absorbing and realizing anthroposophy—of carrying it out into the world. At the same time the attacks of opponents of anthroposophy were becoming increasingly vicious—for example the Goetheanum fire was later proved to have been arson. The many school initiatives claimed Steiner's attention in the absence of enough leaders who were sufficiently versed in Waldorf education and able to deal independently with arising difficulties, particularly among the staff. Also, the commercial enterprises such as Der Kommende Tag (The coming day) which supported firms in loose association, that had been established particularly by the younger members, were running into economic and personal difficulties and many turned to him for help. All this took its toll—it was a difficult and sobering year. But Steiner continued his lecture courses, travelled extensively, and spoke at various conferences throughout the year, wrote several articles, received all those seeking his advice or instruction and initiated the founding of the various national societies—in Norway, Austria, Holland, etc.—which would form the new basis of the General Anthroposophical Society. He visited Great Britain in August, giving a pedagogical course at the conference of the Educational

Union for the Realization of Spiritual Values in Education in Ilkley, Yorkshire. Then on to Penmaenmawr and the summer school organized by D.N. Dunlop. In both places Steiner visited the Druid stone circles nearby with Marie Steiner. Then on to London for further lectures, eurythmy performances and a visit to the Nursery and Training School in Deptford founded by Margaret MacMillan for poor and orphaned children. In addition to all this he was deeply involved in the spiritual research which informed and enriched all his courses on the most disparate subjects such as medicine, theology, art, education and many others.

It is in this context that we should view these lectures, focusing as they do on the decline of European culture, the development of materialism and the gradual loss of access to spirituality. Thinking becomes a mere 'brain sport'. Even Albert Schweitzer is at a loss as to how to overcome the cultural decadence of the times. In the earlier part of the nineteenth century there was a natural access to spirituality as seen for example in the craft associations of the Devorants and Loups Garous in France. It is also significant for European culture that Latin, a dead language, became the lingua franca (sic) of science and particularly of the emerging study of economics! Only those educated in Latin had access to knowledge and those who spoke the vernacular were excluded. This led to a divide in Europe as the East was influenced by Greek and the West by Latin culture.

However, in the last half of the nineteenth century European culture had become so decadent that there was a complete lack of spirituality. Steiner says that materialistic science doesn't even understand matter! This situation forms the background for the development of anthroposophy. As Steiner says here: anthroposophy had no exoteric foundation in European culture on which to build and had to develop without any former groundwork (always excepting the esoteric circles of the Rosicrucians and people like Paracelsus and Jakob Boehme). Importantly however he exhorts anthroposophists not to try through argument to convince natural science of the existence of the spiritual. This cannot be done, materialism is irrefutable. Only if the relevant person is prepared to give up their preconceptions and study anthroposophy is there any point in such discourse. We should remain interested in and tolerant of the world of natural science and indeed of the world at large including those who criticize anthroposophy, but we shouldn't try to convince anyone of spiritual truths. This is only possible when the person in question is prepared to develop their soul in a manner which will prepare them for spiritual perception and enable them to evolve into a conscious spiritual being.

What impressed me in these lectures is how Steiner repeatedly urges us to bring anthroposophy into everyday life, to see how dreams 'protest' against the laws of nature or what a difference there is when we eat and digest a potato for example as compared to a cereal such as rye. And how we can grasp phenomena such as sleepwalking through our understanding of the threefold human being. How our head is the transformed organism of our last life. All eminently down to earth and practical aspects which show us: we can realize spirituality on earth, we can make it real, we can wake up and make anthroposophy real.

And what is truly real? In the last lecture in this volume, he says unequivocally: 'All phenomena outside beings are just illusory; in the cosmos only beings are truly real.' This touched me deeply.

Elizabeth Marshall
Berlin, January 2021

THE NATURE OF THE SPIRITUAL CRISIS OF THE NINETEENTH CENTURY[1]

DORNACH, 5 MAY 1923

TODAY I'd like to examine from another point of view something which has occupied us a great deal recently. I want to look from a historical perspective at the fact that in the last third of the nineteenth century there was in effect a critical transformation in the spiritual life of humanity. This critical change revealed itself through various circumstances. And these circumstances are essentially the basis for what I would call the misery that has taken hold of humanity in the twentieth century; for the foundation of all this misery lies in the spiritual.

But first of all, I'd like to characterize briefly the real essence of the spiritual crisis of the last third of the nineteenth century. In this period there was on the one hand materialism, the materialism of external life, and behind this the materialistic world view. And the idealistic world view had been gradually, and we could almost say shamefacedly, completely abandoned. In the penultimate issue of *The Goetheanum*[2] I've tried to point out the discrepancy between this materialism, which often didn't want to be materialistic but nevertheless was, and idealism. There I briefly sketched how, in the last third of the nineteenth century, idealistic minds, who perpetuated the idealism of the first half of the nineteenth century, played a certain role. And how these minds, these thinkers, precisely because they knew spiritual life only in the form of ideas, couldn't stand their ground in the face of all the arguments being developed on the basis of what natural science was confidently asserting. Natural science, to which there can basically be no objection, was however going beyond its proper purview, as if pure natural science were in a position to make judgements on all the concerns of humanity. At the time in question natural science had its greatest successes, success in relation to cognition, success in relation to external practical, technical life. And all those wishing to repudiate what didn't conform in their opinion to the findings of natural science, could point to these successes.

So, they stood, so to speak, opposite each other: the successful, who could competently explain natural science, but who really only represented materialism, as they still do today, and on the other side those thinkers whose intention was to protect idealism. But these last only knew spiritual life in ideas. They saw, so to speak, behind material beings of the world only ideas and behind the ideas nothing further, no creative spirit. Ideas were for them the ultimate, the last thing they could arrive at. But these ideas are just abstract. They were abstract in the way they were cultivated by these thinkers in the first half of the nineteenth century, and they stayed abstract when they were developed by idealists in the last third of the nineteenth century. And so, these idealists with their abstract ideas, which were for them the only spirit, couldn't hold their ground in the face of the concrete findings of natural science and its concomitant world view.

This is the external historic aspect. But the internal historic perspective lying behind it is something different. And this is that materialism, if it is consistent and spirited—even though materialism denies spirit it can still have great spirit—cannot be disproved. Materialism is irrefutable. It is useless to believe that materialism is a world view that we can disprove. There is no rationale with which we can prove that materialism is wrong. This is why it is a waste of time trying to refute materialism with theoretical arguments.

Why can't materialism be disproved? Now you see, it can't be disproved for the following reasons. Let's take that piece of matter that in human beings themselves is the basis for intellectual activity: the brain or, to go a bit further, the nervous system. This brain or nervous system is an image of the spirit. Everything that exists in the human spirit can be found in one form or another, in one process or another in the brain or the nervous system. So all that we could invoke as an expression of the spirit of the human being can be found reproduced in its material counterpart, in the brain, in the nervous system.

How could someone who points to this nervous system not say: what you really mean when you speak of the soul or the spirit is all these components of the nervous system? It is as if someone looked at a portrait and said: what is pictured here is all there is of the human being, there is no original. If we couldn't find the person whose portrait it is, then perhaps we couldn't prove that there was an original. The portrait alone doesn't provide us with evidence that there is an original. Similarly, the material image of the spiritual world doesn't provide us with evidence that spirit exists. We cannot disprove materialism. There is only the possibility of pointing to the will to find the spirit itself. We must find spirit completely independently of matter, but in doing so we then find it working creatively in matter. However, through descriptions of the material, through conclusions reached through the material, we can never find spirit, because matter consists of images of the spirit.

This is the secret of why in a time such as the last third of the nineteenth century, when people had no direct access to spirit, materialism stood unrefuted, irrefutable, and why, for those who couldn't point to the spirit but only to the abstract, lifeless image of spirit, the ideas in human beings, why these idealistic thinkers couldn't stand their ground against contemporary materialistic thinkers. The dispute couldn't be based on evidence and counter-evidence. It took place under the influence of the power—greater or lesser—of the parties involved in the dispute. And in the last third of the nineteenth century the greater power belonged to those people, who could produce as evidence the progress and successes of natural science with its technical achievements, which convinced by their mere existence.

Of course those people, who as idealistic thinkers such as I've described in the penultimate issue of *The Goetheanum*, preserved the traditions of the first half of the nineteenth century; they were the wiser and more brilliant thinkers, they were the ones whose arguments reached more deeply into people's souls than those of the materialists, but the materialists were more powerful. And the dispute wasn't settled by the evidence, but was a question of power. We only have to face the facts without any illusions. We must be quite clear that in order to reach the spirit we have to seek the way directly and not try to prove its existence through material phenomena. For whatever is in the spirit is also in matter. So, if someone can't find the direct path to the spirit, then they can still find in matter all there is to know of the world.

Since in the last third of the nineteenth century even the most noble minds weren't able to find access to the spirit, but still had spiritual needs and longings, they got into a kind of insecurity about the whole human soul situation. And behind one or other of the really important personalities of the last third of the nineteenth century, their own instability shows up like a backdrop. Even though they were extremely intellectualistic, they were also extremely soulful, so they said to themselves: well, here is the material world, there are the ideas. Ideas are all we can find behind the phenomena of nature and of human beings. But then again, these people feel that ideas are only abstract and lifeless. And so, they slid into uncertainty and instability.

I'd like to demonstrate this through the example of one quite prominent personality, so that you can see in detail how this spiritual development, which ultimately lead to our present era, really was. I'd like to show you the so-called Swabian Vischer[3], who is also called V-Vischer, as he writes his name with a V, unlike all the other academic Fischers—Swabian Vischer, the aesthetician.

He was a product of that whole idealism of the first half of the nineteenth century. He couldn't endorse crude materialism. Everywhere behind material beings and material processes he perceived ideas; basically, he perceived in the moral world order a sum of ideas. He was concerned with discovering the nature of beauty. He sought the nature of beauty in the Hegelian sense, in the idea which shines out of matter as perceived by the senses.

When an artist shapes matter then something ideal shines through the form and it's not just a product of nature, which doesn't reveal an idea; when the artist designs matter, whether it is a metal or musical sounds or words, so that we perceive something ideal in this design, then an idea appears in a sensory form, in a sensory figure, and that is beauty. It's possible that the idea is so powerful, that we experience the sensory object as too impotent to express the greatness of the idea. When for example the sculptor has such a powerful idea that no sensory material can adequately incorporate this idea, so that we can only guess at the immense grandeur behind the form, then beauty becomes sublime. If the idea is too small, so that the artist can play with the material and the idea can express itself in all the genial treatment of the medium, then beauty becomes graceful.

Thus, grace and sublimeness are different forms of beauty. If people sense world harmony in a work created by an artist, then it could be either something sublime or something graceful, according to how the artist has worked. Then we can see how, for example, with Jean Paul, it often turns out that in his representation of world events there is no harmony at all; we see only contradictions everywhere in the world and harmony is something unreachable, hidden behind everything else. However, these world phenomena seem to concern us intimately. We see, for example, a little schoolteacher, with an enormous sense of idealism and a great longing for knowledge, but he has no money to buy books. So, in the second-hand bookshop he asks only for book catalogues instead of books and so he has at least the titles, if not the books themselves. He can at least afford to buy blank paper, so he writes all these books listed by title in the catalogues himself. Then we notice in the poet's subject matter, that there is a certain harmony after all; it's harmonious how he balances out the disharmony caused by the lack of money. But then again, the books that the schoolteacher writes for himself aren't as clever as those in the catalogues. The contradiction still exists. We're thrown back and forth between what should be and what is, but shouldn't be.

If in our soul we can find our way through this intractable conflict, one contradiction following another, where we can't get beyond the conflicts and we wander from one discord to the next, if we can keep calm in our souls, then this is the mood of beauty we savour as humour.

So it was this Swabian Vischer—the V-Vischer—who glorified humour as an aesthetic, because he lived in that time where a helpless humanity was confronted with such conflicts and with the opposition of spirit and matter. Faced with the impossibility of reaching world harmony through human intelligence, he wanted to repair all this through humour. And so, he glorified humour. However, behind it there is always a kind of harmony, without which there could be no humour, otherwise we would notice that we were being jollied along and taken for superficial fools. So behind what Swabian Vischer wanted to enjoy in the world—and he is a leading personality in the second half of the nineteenth century—lies ambition and as it wasn't possible to reach the spiritual in the world, but only ideas, this ambition has something terribly philistine. A snickering humour, behind which in reality there is no soul harmony, but something forced; a humour which, exploring the contradictions in the world, finds not a humoristic reconciliation, but just a foolish jumbling together.

All this is connected to the fact that in the second half of the nineteenth century the more noble minds weren't able to find the spiritual, which is really behind the world, so that they looked for ways of discovering something about it and ended up in a kind of instability and desperation. And this desperation in the last third of the nineteenth century could only lead to the tragic, unhealthy situation of the beginning and first half of the twentieth century.

Now Vischer, having almost tried to resist, still went and put himself (and it is him) on stage in front of the whole world in his novel, *Auch Einer* ('One Too'). The 'hero' of this novel is called Albert Einhart, but Vischer shortens it to A.E. and then calls him 'Auch Einer'. So, the title of the novel is also, *Auch Einer* ('One Too'). Now this 'One Too' is quite ambitious. He wants to be someone, a proper human being, a 'one' or 'One'. He wants to be an individuality in a class of his own, unique. But then, despite his tremendous qualities, he only gets to be not 'One' but just 'One Too'. And as I said Vischer denied that *Auch Einer* is a portrait of his own self. In a sense it's not, but still Vischer has smuggled into the novel the disharmonies in his own soul. And these are the same discrepancies which existed in souls in general in the last third of the nineteenth century.

The novel *One Too* consists of three parts. The first part describes how Vischer gets to know Albert Einhart or 'Auch Einer'. He's an interesting travelling acquaintance, the kind you don't meet every day.

Now you see Vischer had himself not been able to recognize in the fact of the Mystery of Golgotha and its significance for earthly evolution, anything other than the development of an idea. The Christ was for him an abstract idea, which had permeated human evolution. And in reality, on Golgotha in the body of Jesus of Nazareth an abstract idea—Christ—was crucified. Here you can feel how lifeless the concept is. It even harks back to the times of David Friedrich Strauss and the like, when they viewed religion as a collection of images for something that in reality is completely abstract, only ideas. So Christ and the story of Christ should be viewed as images; the emergence of the highest of ideas in earthly evolution, the crucifixion, is only really the appearance of an idea in a highly developed human being and so on. All this was the subject of great intellectual efforts in the nineteenth century and lead to bitter disappointment in all the more profound souls of that time, because behind all these ideas they couldn't find real spirit. And human beings had of course a great thirst for the spirit, as they always do, especially when they have no access to it. And it is those thinkers who believe they can prove that there is no spirit, only matter or ideas, who have the greatest thirst. We could say that at the end of the nineteenth century and the beginning of the twentieth century the greatest minds had become tired of this intellectualistic pursuit of the answer to the questions: how do ideas function in nature? How do abstract ideas affect history? But a mercurial shallow person like Arthur Drews could still produce something, which had basically been discredited among those who were really capable of thinking. And so there survived into the twentieth century in the personality of this mercurial non-thinker, some of this construct: that an idea was crucified and not a real spiritual being.

But from what I've said, you can gather that even for a thinker like Vischer, the spiritual was ultimately dissolved into ideas. In the end these ideas in their abstractness haunted the world like a chimera. Everything we have in mythology or in religion right up until the Christian religion, all this was only at best an image of an idea. Ultimately those people, who strove only to see the idea in the sensory image, came to the conclusion that it doesn't really matter what sensory image we use to express the spinning and weaving of the idea in the material world.

And to such an oddball as Albert Einhart or One Too, who tries to reach the sublime at every opportunity, matter asserts itself in a remarkable way. Whenever he tries to reach the heights of spirituality, which in his case is really only the ideal, he gets catarrh and then he has to sneeze or clear his throat loudly. There matter brings its influence to bear. He never feels matter as strongly as when he has catarrh or even a corn on his foot. If you're such a thinker from the second half of the nineteenth century, you don't really know where to get hold of matter, which produces the images for the ideas. But you could grasp it best where it makes itself felt, where it overcomes the spirit. And in the end you even become like Albert Einhart or One Too, a critic of all that already exists.

Then Albert Einhart has an idea: those people who have only really treated matter in a neutral manner, they've made a mistake. Schiller described William Tell quite wrongly; it's just not possible, matter is treated on much too high a level. We have to go much lower than that. We have to even go into the catarrh, if we really want to grasp matter. And so, the proper composition would be if Tell didn't just reach the other bank in his boat, but capsizes, falls overboard and is rescued by Gessler's men, who then beat him up. Then he escapes, falls into the water again and gets a chill. So now he has a terrible cold and just as he's about to pick up the crossbow he has to sneeze. Gessler, the bailiff, can't say to him: 'That's Tell's shot'. No, he has to say: 'That's Tell's sneeze!' This is how Tell should be, says Albert Einhart, One Too. We have to go more deeply, more fundamentally into materialism if we want to be consistent.

Also there were all sorts of explanations of Othello, psychological interpretations. But Einhart says we should see how Othello is always looking for a handkerchief, that he has a heavy cold that distresses him to such an extent that in the end he strangles Desdemona. Nothing more than a heavy cold! We just have to go more deeply into the material and find the pivotal point.

This is what Vischer with his humorous, soulful outlook is searching for. He can't get beyond materialism. He can't disprove it and so he at least wants to flout it in his soul. He can't flout hydrogen and oxygen but he can definitely defy catarrh. And this is at least a viable attitude towards matter.

All this also leads up to the point where Vischer can reveal how he got to know this strange oddball, Einhart. At the time he is staying in a hotel, which—several things point to this—isn't far from where we are today, somewhere in the mountains. And because he has catarrh, he gets into a spat with the hotel workers and lashes out at one of them. Then suddenly, through this worldly affair, all the regrets of his life are revealed in his soul. And he even goes so far as to want to commit suicide. He tries to throw himself off the mountain. But at this moment Vischer sees him, tries to save him and falls down the mountain himself. Seeing this and forgetting that he wanted to kill himself, Einhart rushes to Vischer's aid. This is how they get to know each other. This is not an everyday kind of acquaintance. They both tumble down the mountainside. And we can hear the curses 'One Too' shouts as he expresses his feelings. In reality we couldn't have heard it, because the sounds of the rushing stream were too loud. But we can hear fragments such as: 'world—a cosmic cold—in solitude—spewing up and world was—coughed up by the eternal—hawked up—brood nest of pest demons'—and so on. Some of it we can hear. Of course, he'll have said a lot more!

Now you've got to know Vischer and his acquaintance 'One Too'. They couldn't communicate well at first as both of them got a cold and had to keep sneezing! So, it took them a bit longer. The first part of the book consists of this rather unusual way of getting to know someone on a journey. The second part is a creation of 'One Too' and consists of the story of a village built on stilts, describing the life of the people living there. We could argue at length about the era in which such villages existed, however there are some clues in the text which lead us to the conclusion that 'One Too' set this stilt village in the area of the town of Turik. This town is situated near here. And at a certain time, the villagers have to call on the services of a young bard from Turik. And this young bard from Turik is called Guffrud Kullur. But we can't really determine when this stilt village existed.

'One Too' tells the story of the stilt village and we learn for example how the villagers provide for their religious needs. And this is exactly the manner in which Vischer and his mirror image, Albert Einhart, view religion: everywhere material images as expressions of ideas. So, one aspect of the religion of the stilt villagers is that there was a time when nobody caught a cold. It was like paradise, as no one could catch a cold. But somehow the villagers weren't quite satisfied with this cold-free, uncatarrhal time and so they fell prey to the temptations of the great god Influenza. This Influenza basically prospers in the cold but works through fire, through overheating. So, from their paradise these stilt villagers fell under the spell of the god Influenza! And they got colds and kept having to sneeze, so then they called upon the witch of the world, who often appears to people as a white cow. You see, another pictorial manifestation, an image of the spiritual. The witch of the world advises them to move the village onto the lake as it gives off a damp, chilly mist. This would drive out the colds. The effects of the god Influenza would be exposed and healed. This would only be possible in a village on stilts.

But then a kind of heretic appears in the village. The villagers have a good leader, a Druid. Although this Druid isn't much cleverer than the other villagers, he has learned to preach the catarrhal religion convincingly and so he controls the whole village. But Druids aren't allowed to marry. So, he doesn't have a wife but a housekeeper, Urhixidur, who in turn dominates him and so has a lot of influence in the village. Now the heretic arrives and wants to teach the villagers a kind of enlightened religion, a religion with no god. However, the villagers have had experience not only of the good gods but also of Influenza and so on. And the Druid, goaded on by Urhixidur, sets up a court of inquisition. The villagers were starting to despair of their Druid as he had instigated the building of a new stilt village deeper in the lake, but he can't explain why. So now they call in Guffrud Kullur from the nearest town and then another scholar, Feridan Kallar. Now the interesting thing is that when a stilt village was excavated, not in Turik but in another Swiss town, one of the investigators was Ferdinand Keller[4], who came not from there but from Turik. Just as the author doesn't allude to Gottfried Keller, but to Guffrud Kullur. So now there is a struggle between those people with the original religion, those with the catarrhal religion and the heretic, who wants to teach a religion with no god, a religion based on a moral world order. These are interesting battles. They escalate when the stilt villagers celebrate a sacrament corresponding to the Catholic or Protestant confirmation, the feast of the handkerchief, whereby the children are brought into the church community. But of course, according to village beliefs they receive not what children are normally given at their confirmation, but a handkerchief. They need a proper handkerchief to help them on their life's path.

All sorts of cultural struggles are going on. According to 'One Too', these cultural wars weren't just raging in the world at large but also in the stilt village.

So, it seems to me that Vischer was trying through a kind of forced humour to describe this situation of not really being able to deal with materialism. I think in his heart he meant that whether in the end we accept those concepts developed by the materialistic art historians, which ultimately stem from a neutral kind of materialism, or others which are more explicit in their materialism isn't important. What is important is to realize that both are materialistic concepts.

Gottfried Semper[5] however argues that when we want to explain the one or other architectural style, what is important is the working of the stone, the workability of the wood. But why should our focus be on the workability of the wood or the stone? Why should we start out from this material aspect? It's much more intelligent to look at how people are affected by the various architectural styles, then we'd have the connection of these styles with the human being and with human evolution. The Greeks had this; their architectural style was open on all sides, so that if you spent a lot of time in these build-ings, you ended up with a proper cold. Those antique styles are pure catarrhal architecture. But in the Gothic buildings you were more protected, you only caught a cold when you opened the windows: so, they were hybrid catarrhal architectural styles. And the ideal is in the remote future: those are the buildings in which you never catch a cold. You can differentiate it nicely—this is how they do it in scholarly texts:

- architectural style A: pure catarrhal
- architectural style B: hybrid catarrhal
- architectural style C: where you never catch a cold.

This is the classification of styles according to *One Too*.

So you see, Vischer didn't know what position to take regarding materialism. He wanted to do it with humour and so he seized on that aspect of materialism, where human beings really feel their materialistic manifestation. This is what in fact lies behind the novel, *One Too*.

In the third part we have aphorisms written by Albert Einhart and so we get to know him better. We learn of his struggle with nature, his struggle with the spiritual, with the moral world order, with pure idealism. These aphorisms are quite witty. Sometimes we even get the impression that the rather pedantic Vischer has anticipated the ingenious ideas of Friedrich Nietzsche. There is really something quite extraordinarily clever in these aphorisms of Albert Einhart.

Albert Einhart is quite an original personality. As we make his acquaintance in the novel he's already retired, as he was something in the order of a police commissioner, a person of some importance. Vischer obviously wants to make the point that this alone is something to be taken with humour: an important police commissioner. But because he was important, he was once elected to the chamber of deputies as a representative and there he gave an important speech. In this speech the first fiery sentence is followed by a second fiery sentence, which however acts like an extinguisher on the first sentence. It's quite remarkable how the second sentence pours cold water on the first. Now there are people present who belong to terrible old, barbaric times and who want to see corporal punishment in the military and in the schools. This leads us back to those times before idealism, when there was no metaphorical religion, when there was only a sheer moral agenda, religion without a god. In our times we shouldn't embrace this kind of thing. In our times there should be no corporal punishment; indeed, we should completely eradicate corporal punishment. And there are a number of other things that should be eradicated now too. We see here how barbarism still raises its head in our age. We can see how on the street cruel people torture animals, for example horses, which aren't made to be whipped. Or we see how dogs, which don't have hooves, but whose feet are differently constructed and not made for pulling carts, still have to pull carts. In short, we see how animals are cruelly treated and I want to bring forward a motion here in the chamber that all who are cruel to animals will be publicly whipped!

When the second fiery spark pours over the first like an extinguisher, then only a certain humour will come to our aid. This Albert Einhart, this 'One Too', is a real creature of the last third of the nineteenth century! And much of what Vischer himself felt as conflicts in his own soul, he brought out in the person of 'One Too'. But again, we shouldn't identify Vischer with 'One Too', nor with the person who arrives in the stilt village as a heretic and was put before the court of inquisition, otherwise we would arrive at some weird conclusions.

Vischer had himself, not in Turik but in another town, officiated in a kind of heretic protectorate and it didn't do him any good. But we must beware of such interpretations and of getting into an overly humorous position with regard to Vischer. For Vischer himself didn't want to accept the second part of Goethe's *Faust* and he mocked the commentators, the interpreters, by writing a third part of *Faust*, in which he refers to those who commentated so brilliantly on the second part as *Deutobold Allegoriowitsch Mystificinsky (Interpretchik Allegoriewitch Mystificinsky)*. Or *Symbolizetti*. And under these names he wrote the third part of Goethe's *Faust*, satirizing the commentators who saw in it a deeper wisdom. Now we don't want to end up as an 'Allegoriewitch' by falling into the trap of interpreting *One Too* as being the story of Vischer's own life.

I think it's remarkable how in this last third of the nineteenth century we have on the one hand the deeply tragic Nietzsche, who was ruined by the contradictions which tore apart his soul, and on the other, Vischer, who couldn't help but express the untenability of contemporary world views in the way he did in his novel, *One Too*. We could say there is even a kind of unity in this novel, as there is a kind of unity in certain materialistic attitudes of natural science. Because if you look at hydrogen, or at oxygen, at zinc or at gold, they are all different, but you will find a kind of unity at the atomic level. They all consist of atoms, just put together in different ways, so that they produce different things. And here in this novel there's also a curious unity.

For example, 'One Too' had had an encounter with a woman, whom he greatly admired, and then he meets her again when she's become a widow. It's a big moment for him. He owes the husband a great debt of gratitude for having died! He finds this person whom he admires so much, as a widow in a hotel. They strike up a conversation. But this conversation is interrupted because 'One Too' has a terrible fit of sneezing. They can't finish their conversation. It's always the material world which hinders him, which rebels against his search for a life philosophy, for the spiritual; it's always the material, which interferes and turns everything ultimately into matter. We can't help but sign up to materialism, when we are just about to express the most sublime feelings of the human soul and then we can't even finish the word 'ideal', but just start 'id…' and end up in a long sneeze! Here we see how matter asserts itself everywhere and how the ideal just disappears in the face of the material.

This novel, *One Too* by Vischer is a significant contribution to cultural history, even though we must admit that a lot of it is quite superficial. On the other hand, this is also an adequate expression of the times. And it expresses exactly that as a spiritually minded person you could find no orientation for the needs of the human soul in the intellectual and material developments of the time. In your thinking you could only arrive at the most abstract ideas, as did 'One Too', which then contradicted themselves as did the abolition of cruelty to animals by whipping the perpetrators! The one idea kills the other. And if you turned to matter, you got it exactly where it was easiest to see: in the nasal mucus.

Even though it wasn't very dignified, Vischer had still written a very interesting book about frivolity and cynicism. He never wanted to be frivolous and hated the tightly laced waists of the women of the times, but he still found something appropriate about cynicism, which he felt obliged to use to describe things effectively. So that's why he didn't shy away from describing worldly events in a materialistic sense, if not frivolously, at least in an unappetizing, but for his taste humoristic, manner.

We have to try to grasp what lives in the various times not just through abstract thoughts or through sentimentality, but in the atmosphere of those times. And I do think that some of the atmosphere of the last third of the nineteenth century lived in the soul of this man Vischer, as he wrote his novel, *One Too*.

The Mystery of The Head and of the Lower Human Being

DORNACH, 6 MAY 1923

WHEN we look at a phenomenon like that we were speaking of yesterday, we see clearly that in the last third of the nineteenth century there was not only the rise of materialism, but also of something which was basically worse, a certain insecurity and instability in those thinkers, who couldn't go all the way with materialism. In the last third of the nineteenth century we find the following elements. We find that those people who were really materialistic in their attitude already had a certain inner assurance. We only need to take a look at those people, who out of a position of knowledge and power declared the findings of natural science far superior and proceeded to establish a whole world view thereon. They presented this with enormous aplomb. And it wasn't so much the content of what they said, as the certainty with which they presented it, that at the time recruited so many followers to materialism. In contrast, all those who could only uphold the spiritual in the form of abstract ideas, felt as insecure as did Vischer, about whom I spoke yesterday. They could only hold on to the spiritual by saying: behind the phenomena of the sensory world ideas are at work. But they could only present these ideas abstractly. They couldn't show people the real spiritual life behind these ideas. Indeed, as these abstract ideas didn't have the power to guide them, they weren't able to speak about real spiritual life. And so as early as the 1890s there was nothing left in public life of the idealism that had still been important in the first half of the nineteenth century, where it was represented by only a few people, as I mentioned in the penultimate issue of *The Goethe-anum*[6], until by the turn of the century it had all but disappeared.

It's characteristic that at the start of the last third of the nineteenth century a book was published that became very influential: *History of Materialism* by Friedrich Albert Lange. This book made a deep impression at the time, appearing in 1866 and so ushering in the last third of the nineteenth century. We can understand this *History of Materialism* as a symptom of the soul-condition humanity was then in the process of developing. Now what does this book say?

Friedrich Albert Lange describes roughly how human beings couldn't develop a more reasonable world view than materialism and if they wanted to avoid being victims of illusion, there was no other possible view than to declare atomistic matter as the basis of all knowledge. So, we have to take this atomic world of matter spread out in space as the basis of reality.

Friedrich Albert Lange noticed however that we have to develop concepts of this world and that these concepts or ideas are not the same as what exists in atoms. But he said: now concepts are a fiction, a play on words, and he coined the phrase: conceptual poetry. So human beings produce these fictions as needed. However, there is the problem that humans don't each produce their own fiction, but that they tend to produce collective concepts, which everyone understands. But for him the concepts are fiction and only atomic matter scattered throughout space is real. So you see, this is crass materialism, which declares that anything going beyond materialism is just fiction. We could say that at least he has a consistent point of view! Unfortunately, that's not the case in Lange's book. If only he'd gone as far as I've just said, then he'd be a consistent materialist. Fine. As I said yesterday, we can't refute materialism if it's consistent. And if someone has no access to the spiritual world—and this is surely true of Lange—then they basically have no choice but to establish materialism as the only valid world view.

But Lange doesn't do this; instead he says something else, which runs like a thread through all the arguments in his book. He says that it's right to assume that the material atomic world is the real world.

But when you assert this, when you say that the material atomic world is at work in space, subdivided into hydrogen, nitrogen, which combine in certain ways and so on, when these ideas are developed in the brain, then that is ultimately also conceptual poetry. Thus materialism, which we necessarily have to endorse, is itself really only an idealism, just as the atomic world is itself a fiction.

We can express what Lange presents in his world-famous book in a much simpler way, in a much simpler image. This is namely the well-known personality of Muenchhausen, who pulls himself out of the mire by his own hair. The idealist pulls himself out of the mire and into materialism by his own idealistic hair.

So we see that one of the most world-famous works at the beginning of the last third of the nineteenth century is just plain, ordinary nonsense—we really can't call it anything else but nonsense. If this *History of Materialism* were materialistic, then it would at least be something new. But that it's a fictional materialism—that's just nonsense.

So what was going on in the last third of the nineteenth century, which had such success with natural science? We have to look at the historical facts. What's going on? Lange's book becomes world-famous, as it's translated into all the leading languages of the time and the most distinguished, enlightened minds hailed it as a liberating work.

You may know the poem by Christian Morgenstern[7] in its eurythmic form, where the one sound, Bim, flies over Bam, and joins up with Bum. 'He's a good Christian but that's just it.'

You have to remember all those people who based their thinking on Lange and who then provided the basis for our whole official world view. These were all enlightened thinkers—at least for the last third of the nineteenth century! And those who were just the audience for all this didn't notice anything amiss. And so, for those issues which touch on the deepest questions of humanity, they were all fast asleep.

You will probably say this is an exaggeration. But it's not an exaggeration! No, it's more of an understatement, when I speak of how deeply asleep all those people were with regard to the greatest questions of spiritual life. What I've said isn't exaggerated, rather in this case public opinion is completely deficient. If we want to develop a healthy basis for a future spiritual life, then we have to face up squarely to these difficult facts as I've just described them. Because through what happened then, humanity's interest in the spiritual world was cut off, people were cut off from spiritual development. And subsequently the less someone touched on spiritual problems, the more people regarded them as a great scientist. That was the situation at the turn of the century.

This is the situation that what was to become anthroposophy was faced with. And this is how we have to understand the task of anthroposophy. We have to understand it as having to work from the ground up and not building on previous work in the one or the other direction. There is nothing there and so we have to understand the essence of anthroposophy from the ground up. For if we do this, we'll find that the facts that exist through the work of natural science are extremely useful for anthroposophic research and indeed these scientific facts will only be properly understood through anthroposophic research. This is the way we have to look at the situation. However, for this to happen some of humanity must resolve to transform intellectualism into the spiritual.

Of course, those people who align themselves with the anthroposophic movement are all filled with a certain impulse, a certain disposition for the spiritual world. But only very few of them want to be bothered with bringing the contemporary world of ideas into the spiritual. Many people want to exclude the world of ideas and to absorb anthroposophy as a kind of comfort for the soul. But this won't be enough to give anthroposophy the power of impulse it needs for the life of the mind. You see what we need here has to be grasped individually and practically and so today I want to give you an individual and practical example.

I have often said, that what you have today as a head on your shoulders is the transformed organism of your past life, except that you have to imagine that in this organism of your last life the head isn't there. Truly, we have to eliminate the head from what we were in our last life—it dissolves into space. And the rest of the organism becomes the head in the next life. Then the organism of that life becomes the head of the next earthly life and so on.

Now someone could say, but it wasn't only my head that was buried at the end of my last life, the rest of my organism was buried too. It didn't have the opportunity to evolve into the head for my present earthly life. Now that's a very superficial understanding. There you're not looking at your head or at the rest of the organism, you're only looking at the physical matter which fills your head today. And this matter transforms itself in the course of earthly life approximately every seven years. What your body has today as matter, didn't exist eight years ago. What goes through earthly life is the invisible, supersensible form.

Of course, you've incorporated the material, which now fills out your head, in this earthly life. But the form, the supersensible forces, which today round out the eyes and turn up the nose, these are the same forces which formed your arms and legs and the rest of the organism in your last earthly life. That other people can see you with their physical senses is due to the fact that matter, which has no form of its own, fills out your form. It's not matter which gives you your form. When you eat salt, it still wants to be crystalline, it doesn't want to be in the shape of a nose or an eye. That you have the form you have as a human being is not due to matter, although it is the reason for your being visible. But the present form of your head has been through a metamorphosis originating in the form of your organism without the head in your last earthly life. Because of this, however, your head was in a very advantageous situation and was well-treated by the cosmos. Therefore, the head appears first in its nearly finished form in the embryo. Think of it: in the embryo the head is practically finished, while the rest of the organism almost hangs off it like a secondary organ. This rest still has to be fashioned from the outside and looks awful in comparison to the fully developed human form, while the head is beautifully made from the beginning. For someone who only values the fully grown human being however, the head of the embryo has a repugnant aspect, but really, it's very well-formed. This is because it brings with it some of its formative forces from an earlier life.

The head has been worked on between death and a new birth as I've described in the lectures on cosmology, religion and philosophy[8] some time ago in the Goetheanum. This work between death and a new birth has to do with the development of the formative forces of the human head.

This is the reason why, in relation to the cosmos, the human head is extraordinarily well-developed. The human head actually contains the material image of the spirit, soul and body of that person. Thus, when we look at the head, we then have the interaction of spirit, soul and body in a material way, insofar as they appear in material form. We could say that for the human head, spirit, soul and body are physical. The secret of the human head is that here the spirit appears in physical form and we can demonstrate this materially in the miracle of the brain. This miraculous structure is an image of the spirit. Just as sealing wax takes the impression of the signet ring, so in the head we have spirit, soul and body in material form.

For the human metabolic-limb system, we can say that everything is physically present. The legs, these two columns, don't have any of the miraculous nature of the human head. They have yet to go through this metamorphosis. They will appear as the lower jaw with all its wonderful functions and mobility in the next earthly life, while after the transformation the arms appear in the upper jaw and so on. In the musculoskeletal system—though the arms have adapted to the upright posture—the opposite is true: there spirit, soul and body are spiritual. There spirit, soul and body are completely spiritual.

We could almost say that the appearance of the human being in relation to the legs and all that is associated with them isn't the true one. This will all reveal itself in its true material form in the next life, when it's become the head. Now it's just at the beginning and how it now appears isn't really its essential form. Its essence is what it becomes when it's directed by the will: humans transform their loco-motor system into will in movement, dynamics, statics. This part of the human being is spiritually intangible, supersensible. The head of every material being is an image of the spiritual and the spirit itself appears there in matter, whereas in the locomotor system the body is hardly physical. If we want to find the meaning of the whole of the locomotor system, we have to explore how much the physical reveals of the spiritual. Thus, we can say that the great mystery of the head is that spirit, soul and body are physical. And the great mystery of the lower part of the human being is that spirit, soul and body are spiritual.

The Old Testament knew from instinctive clairvoyance much more about these things than modern humanity. Modern humanity overestimates the head. I've already discussed this from various perspectives. In the Old Testament you'll never find the illusory view that the brain concocts dreams! There it says that Jehovah tormented someone in their sleep in relation to their kidneys[9]. In those days they knew that what appears in dreams is from the metabolic system. They didn't ascribe everything to the head. Why do people attribute everything to the head these days? I have to say it's because no one believes in the spirit and so they don't look at that part of the human being where even the body's still spiritual. They don't look at the lower human being, because they're not proud of it. So, they look there, where even the spirit is physical-material, they look at the head. They're proud of it because here spirit becomes material-physical.

Overestimating the head, that's materialism. People only want matter and they only want the spirit as matter. This is the reason we find the head described in the way it is in our modern physiological, scientific works, because they only want spirit in a material way. And this is true, but only in the head. But of course, they know nothing of the fact that before this head could bring down the spirit into its material, physical-image form, it had to go through this whole life between death and a new birth. And that in order for this material image of the human spirit to appear in the form of the head, it had first to go through a long spiritual development. This material miracle of the human brain is the result of a wonderful spiritual development. But people only want to look at the material, only want to accept the spirit in its material form.

Now my dear friends, we should really pay attention. Even if we're over 14 we can still pay attention. In the human being we have a region up here that is completely physical and a region down here that is completely spiritual. However, shouldn't there be an area in the middle which is neither completely physical nor completely spiritual, that is both or neither? In the middle there must be a neutral point where the spiritual flows into the physical and the physical into the spiritual. A place where neither of them are dominant, where the human being is neither dependent on the upper region nor on the lower. A place somewhere in the middle, where we are independent of both.

It is important to understand this point, which must be located in the middle of the human being, in our chest area. Imagine that you have a pair of scales. Imagine that you have a load on the one side and balancing weights on the other: now you balance it out. If you put more weight on the one side, then it goes down and the same on the other side. Also, you can't remove anything without disturbing the balance. So, you see, in the middle there's a point, a neutral point. You can add as much as you like to this point, it won't change the balance of the scales. You could even take hold of the scales themselves here and, if you avoid creating an imbalance by swinging them around, then you can move them any which way without disturbing the balance. You can balance the scales while you are actually moving them around. This is a point which doesn't affect the whole system of the scales, a point of balance. You can practically do with it what you like, it doesn't change anything in the functioning of the scales. For example, someone puts a load on here and weights on the other side. Now it occurs to him that the arm of the scales is made of iron, which he doesn't like, so he wants to have it in gold. Now he only needs to expand the midpoint somewhat; even though it's a mathematical point you can still expand it a bit. You could put gold in the fulcrum if you so wished and it wouldn't change the balance at all. If you put the gold somewhere else, for example outside the midpoint, then the balance changes. Otherwise even if someone wanted to make a hollow space in the fulcrum and put meat in it, that wouldn't change the balance either. Someone else would prefer butter, which then melts in the sun, but the balance of the scales is not affected. In short, this point is completely independent of the whole system of the scales. You can't affect it.

It's the same with the point which lies as a balance in the middle between the physical and the spiritual. This point is dependent neither on the physical nor on the spiritual. Human beings can make of this point whatever they want.

If you think that humans are merely physical beings and everything is just a result of cause and effect, then you won't find this point. Or if you think that humans are merely spiritual beings and everything is determined by the divine worlds, then here too there is nothing you can do about it, as humans just have to do what the gods have decided. But if we know that above a certain point of balance humans are determined by the gods and below it by the material world, then we see that with this one point, which we can trace to the middle of the human being, we can do whatever we want in the world out of our own free will. If you then have this threefold human constitution you can recognize in the centre the scientifically proven fact of human freedom. We can safely say that it's as scientific as the solution to any mathematical equation or derivative. It's something that can be treated with the strictest rules of science. Freedom is the result of a genuine knowledge of the human constitution, because in human beings there's a point which is as independent of the upper part and of the lower part of their constitution as the pivotal point of the scales is independent of the load to the right and left of it. You can carry the scales around with you, you can even replace this point as I said earlier with anything you want. And you can find a point in the human being where natural causality, cause and effect, ceases and where the correlation with the heavens, the determination through the spiritual world also ceases and where there is a balance between the two. Here in the pivotal point of human nature is the guarantee of human freedom. And we can prove it in the strict scientific sense with a true physiology and a true psychology; but not of course with those we have today, which, as I have already shown, become completely dilettantish in psychoanalysis.

This is something that should make people think. You can take all of literature and philosophy and read everywhere on the issue, but nobody really gets to grips with the problem of freedom. Why is this? It's because nobody has a true concept of the human being. This is only possible today through anthroposophy. And the fact that nobody can really deal with the problem of freedom refers back to what I was talking about, albeit in a humorous fashion, yesterday. What I was trying to show yesterday with the help of what was meant to be a humorous novel, I could have also presented in a serious manner.

It is important to treat these things earnestly if we want to be serious about anthroposophy. Then it's really a question of understanding actual realities and applying them in the appropriate way. And if you don't really know, whether you should acknowledge the spiritual, when you only know spirit in abstract ideas, or should you endorse materialism, then you would become a humourist like Vischer. And like Vischer you would develop a humorous world system, the catarrhal system. Of course, we can laugh about it, but we can't say with absolute certainty that the world wasn't created by a 'divine sneeze'. Here he isn't using the material world in the right way. That's the whole point, we have to use the material in the right way. Whether we want to understand it or to apply it we have to use it in the right way. Yesterday I gave you an example in the way Vischer sees the world and how he creates a whole world system out of this catarrh, as if it were an imperative, an overpowering reality. We don't do this in anthroposophy! I acted as if I had a cold yesterday, coughing occasionally, but that was only as an illustration and not to form the basis of a whole philosophy.

If you stagger helplessly from a catarrhal materialism to a spirit consisting only of ideas, then you will end up talking about being seduced by the great God Influenza. This isn't possible in anthroposophy. Here we promote a remedy for flu, so as not to be tempted to make up a whole myth of original sin around the great God Influenza! It's a case of understanding the material world in the right way and assigning it to its proper place.

Things have to change enormously. Someone with a mind like Vischer in the last third of the nineteenth century was angry, coughing and sneezing, and ended up inventing the charade about the great God Influenza. As an anthroposophist you would try to cure the flu with our remedy[10], which is quite effective. This shows you what a difference it makes when you treat the material from a spiritual point of view.

However, the contemporary cognitive view of the head shows that in the modern philosophy of the world there is a deep sympathy with materialism. And the fact that nobody can really come to an understanding of the problem of freedom, shows that they don't know that impulses from two different worlds are at work on the upper and on the lower human being respectively. Those minds that in years gone by focussed on the upper part found that humans can't be free as everything is preordained by the spiritual world. All those who study humanity today ascribe everything to a simple natural causality. From both points of view human beings cannot be free. Spiritual causality is valid for the head and natural causality for the metabolic-limb system. In between there lies the rhythmic organization, which is rhythmic because here everything balances out rhythmically. In the rhythmic organization there is something which is determined neither by the spiritual nor the material, is neither preordained nor the result of cause and effect, and is the point from which the freedom impulse originates.

You see how in such a practical way we can show how anthroposophy casts light on the deepest problems of humanity. In my book, *Riddles of the Soul* I presented the nature of the human being as three-membered: the nerve-sense system, the rhythmic system and the metabolic-limb system. At the same time this referred back to the *Philosophy of Freedom*, in which freedom is simply presented as a fact. This reference to freedom as a fact was meant as follows: if you see human beings in their true essence as having a three-membered organization, then you can arrive at a scientifically exact description of human freedom. This would be the same process as you would use to arrive at a description of the pivotal point of a set of scales or of any system of forces, a point which is independent of the interaction of the forces in the system. But you would also see how today you can look wherever you want, nowhere will you find any truth about these things. So, based on all these inadequate concepts, which are wholly unrelated to the true nature of human organization, we educate our children and develop moral, religious and social systems. Then it's no surprise when these social systems produce such monstrous thinking as was described by Leinhas in the recent

Goetheanum[11]. There someone had to admit that the ideas associated with Marxism had disproved themselves in real life, but that wasn't really important; we would have to wait until someone could prove it scientifically. Really you can only quote these words in inverted commas exactly as the source said them, because if you think them through for yourself, your head threatens to explode. Not only does a mill wheel start turning in your brain, you feel as if your head will burst, when you try to think something like that through.

Therefore, it's important to not just move in anthroposophic circles and to cold-shoulder all that's going on outside, but to have an interest for how chaotic all our contemporary thinking is and all that has developed from it in the outside world.[12]

Cultural Phenomena

DORNACH, 1 JULY 1923

Today's lecture is intended as a special episode in the series I've been giving, because it's important that anthroposophists are well and truly awake and can form their own opinion by observing the world in a certain way. Therefore in between those lectures concerned with anthroposophic material, it's essential that we occasionally include one dealing with the state of our civilization and what is going on in the wider world. So today I want to expand on something I already described in an article in *The Goetheanum*, where I spoke about a newly published text: 'The decline and restoration of civilization' by Albert Schweitzer[13]. It's presented as the first part of a philosophy of civilization and deals basically with a critique of contemporary culture. I'd like to start with a single, but very typical, example of this contemporary culture in order to provide a solid basis for what Albert Schweitzer is describing. There are thousands to choose from. You only need to take something at random from modern cultural life—you could say cultural death—and you will find enough examples. As I mentioned in the educational lectures yesterday and today[14], it's really a question of getting used to observing such things honestly and directly. So as an illustration I've chosen something which is always a good representation of contemporary culture, the inaugural speech of the rector of a Berlin university held on the 15 October 1910[15]. This rector is a physician, a person not beholden to any particular philosophical view of culture, who wanted to give a kind of overview of modern scientific thinking.

Now I don't want to bother with the first part of the speech, which is mainly about the university, but to acquaint you with the general world view that this Doctor Rubner presented at the inaugural ceremony. This example is perhaps typical as it comes from the year 1910, when all of Europe and beyond believed, optimistically enough, that there was an enormous intellectual boom, a flood of intellectual achievements. What I want to pick up on is a kind of aside to the students, which allows us to gain insight into just what such a representative of his time was concerned with in his soul. First he speaks to the students as follows: 'We all have to learn. We bring nothing into the world but an instrument for intellectual activity, a blank page, our brain, with various talents and different potentials for development; we receive everything from the world around us.'

Obviously if someone grows up in this modern materialistic culture, they can hold this view. We shouldn't be mean-spirited. We have to be clear what power this materialistic culture exercises on contemporary people and we can understand why someone would speak about coming into the world with the brain as a blank page and receiving everything from the world environment. But let's listen to the rest of what he has to say to the students. He continues the argument that we are all blank pages and how the child of even the most distinguished mathematician still has to learn their times table, because unfortunately they don't inherit mathematics from their father; then how the child of the greatest linguist still has to learn their native language and so on. No brain wants to have to comprehend all that their ancestors have experienced and learnt. But here he advises those very brains consisting of blank pages on what they have to do in the world to become inscribed. He continues: 'What millions of brains in the course of human history have pondered and developed, all that our intellectual heroes have created...' and so on. This goes on for two whole pages; he wants to impress it on them. They come with a brain as a blank page and they have to strive to absorb all that these intellectual heroes have created.

But if these intellectual heroes were all blank pages, where has all that they created, which the new blank pages are supposed to absorb, come from? What a strange way of thinking! These blank-page brains, he goes on: 'receive in the form of short sentences during their education what our intellectual heroes have created and from this they can develop their own character and their individual life'.

Next, he presents these blank-page brains with a remarkable sentence: 'What you've learnt gives you the raw material for productive thinking.' So suddenly productive thinking appears in the unwritten pages of these brains. It should be self-evident, for someone who contends that brains are unwritten pages, that they can't simultaneously expect productive thinking.

This is the kind of sentence which shows just how materialistically even the best minds thought. Rubner isn't one of the worst. He's a doctor and has even read the philosopher Zeller[16], and that's quite something! He's not at all small-minded, you see. But how does he think? He wants to depict the freshness of life and so he says: 'It's always very refreshing to start work on a new unploughed field of the brain.' So when the student has learnt something and then later goes on to another subject, this means that they're ploughing a new field in the brain. You see the thought forms have a typical materialistic tone. He goes on: 'Some brain fields only yield up their fruits when they've been worked repeatedly, but then their yield is as good as other fields which don't have to be worked so hard.'

It's very difficult to follow this thinking, because first the brain is supposed to be a blank page, but then it has to learn everything from brains with inscribed pages, who however must themselves have been blank at birth. Now this brain has to be ploughed. But there would at least have to be a ploughman present! The more we try to follow this incredible, impossible thinking, the more bewildered we become. However, Max Rubner is concerned about his students and so he advises them to plough their brains thoroughly. Now he can't help but say that thinking is what ploughs the brain. So, he has to recommend thinking. But now his materialistic thought really goes to town and he finds the lovely sentence: 'Thinking strengthens the brain; training enhances its performance just as it does any organ, just as our muscle strength is enhanced through work and sport. Studying is brainsport.'

So now the Berlin students of 1910 knew what thinking is: 'Thinking is brainsport.' However, it doesn't even occur to this representative of contemporary culture what is really interesting about sport, much more interesting than what goes on on the outside. It's much more interesting to look at what actually goes on in people's limbs when they do different sports, what's going on on the inside. Then we'd find something really interesting. If we looked at sport in this way, we would discover that sport is one of those activities belonging to the metabolic-limb aspect of human organization. Thinking belongs to the nerve-sense organization. There everything is turned on its head. What in the human being is turned towards the inside, the inner processes, are in thinking turned towards the outside. And what goes outwards in sport, goes inwards in thinking. This means when we consider thinking we have to allow for this. But this representative of contemporary culture has forgotten how to think and so he can't think any thought through to the end.

Our whole modern culture has emerged from this unfinished, unresolved type of thinking. We can capture the essence of this thinking in such representatives of modern culture. We catch it there, so to speak, red-handed. Unfortunately, it's rare for someone to notice this. When the rector of a Berlin university gives an inaugural speech entitled 'Our goals for the future', it's a solemn moment for a truly modern person. It's what science says; it's what the invincible authority of science, which knows everything, says. And if science has proven that thinking is brainsport, then we have to just accept that. Then humans have become clever enough after all these centuries to realize that thinking is brainsport.

I could go on with these observations and look at the most diverse fields and we would see that everywhere the same—I can't say spirit— the same non-spirit rules. Now some people with a deeper insight had seen this before the decadence was externally visible. And we have as an example Albert Schweitzer, who wrote the excellent book *The Quest of the Historical Jesus from Reimarus to Wrede*, which in its keen, thoughtful, thorough and profound thinking could at least get as far as the apocalypse in its research on the life of Jesus. We could rely on Schweitzer to have a clear view of the decadence of contemporary culture. Now he assures us that his book, *The Decay and Restoration of Civilisation*[17] wasn't written after the war, but that the first draft was ready in 1900 and the final version was written in 1914 to 1917. Now it's been published. And here is someone looking at the decline of modern civilization with their eyes open. It's always interesting to see how such an observer of cultural decline works with sharp tools on our civilization. Indeed, some of his sentences about modern culture do seem as cutting as knives. Let's have a look at a few of these. This is the first sentence in the book:

> We stand at the brink of the fall of civilization. The war is not the cause of this situation. The war is itself one of the signs. What was already a spiritual reality has now become fact, which in turn affects the spiritual undoubtedly for the worse. We abandoned civilization because we had no way of thinking about it. Thus, we crossed the threshold of the century with unchallenged illusions about ourselves. Now it's obvious to everyone that our culture is in the process of destroying itself.

Although he does tend to praise himself for it, still Albert Schweitzer sees that the decline of civilization began in the middle of the nineteenth century, which I have often described as an important moment to look at if we want to clearly understand the present. Schweizer says about this time:

> Around the middle of the nineteenth century the discussions of ethical ideals, reason and reality had subsided and in the course of the next few decades they practically disappeared. The abdication of civilization went ahead without a fight, without a whimper. Culture's thinking lagged behind the times as if it were too exhausted to keep pace.

And he has another, somewhat surprising argument, which we can however understand quite well, having often talked about it here, albeit in a deeper sense than is meant by Schweitzer. For him it's clear: in earlier times there was a complete world view. All the phenomena of life from the mineral down below up to the highest human ideals were all part of a life totality. The divine-spiritual being was at work in this life totality. If you wanted to know how natural laws functioned, then you turned to the divine-spiritual being. If you wanted to know how moral laws or religious laws functioned, then you turned to the divine-spiritual being. There existed a total world view, where morality was as anchored in objectivity as natural laws are anchored in objectivity. The last world philosophy to emerge, which still had something of this total world view was the Enlightenment, which wanted to derive everything from reason, but still made an inner connection between morality and the natural world.

Consider how often I've said this here: if today someone believes honestly in natural laws, then they have to believe in a world-beginning similar to that described by the Kant-Laplace theory and in the end of the world as it would be in a heat death. Then we have to imagine that all ethical ideals are boiled out of the chaos of cosmic nebulae, which then slowly mass together and become crystals and organisms and ultimately human beings. Then ethical ideals start to flow out of these humans. But these ethical ideals are only illusions, born out of the swirling atoms of the human being and they will disappear when the earth disappears into the heat death. This means that a philosophy develops, which only relates to nature and in which there is no anchorage for moral ideals. And it's only because modern humans are so dishonest and unable to admit this, that they deny the facts and still believe that moral ideals have some kind of anchorage. But whoever believes in modern science and is honest with themselves, can't believe in the eternalness of moral ideals. If someone does so nevertheless, then this is craven dishonesty. We have to look at our present time with no illusions.

Albert Schweitzer sees this too, in his own way, and he looks for the reasons behind it. He says: 'The failure of philosophy was crucial.' Now we can all have our own ideas about this and you could think that philosophers were like the hermits of the world and the rest of humanity has nothing to do with them. But Schweitzer rightly says in another passage in his text: 'Kant and Hegel have ruled over millions of people, who have never read them and didn't even know they were following them.' The paths that world thoughts take are not as we imagine them to be. I myself am a witness to the fact that until the end of the nineteenth century Hegel's most important works stood on the library shelves and the pages weren't even cut open. Nobody was studying them. But those copies that a few people read exerted an enormous influence on contemporary cultural life. And there's hardly anybody here today whose thinking hasn't been influenced by Kant and Hegel. As I said, these paths are mysterious. And if in the most remote mountain village people are at least reading newspapers, then they're also ruled by Kant and Hegel. So, it's not just true of the present illustrious and learned audience sitting in this room!

Thus we can say with Albert Schweitzer:

> The failure of philosophy was crucial. In the eighteenth and the beginning of the nineteenth century philosophy was the leader of public opinion. Philosophy was concerned with the condition of humanity and the questions of the time and encouraged people to think about these things. So, at that time there was an elementary philosophical debate about humanity, society and culture, which naturally produced a popular philosophy, that dominated public opinion and cultural interests.

And now Schweitzer argues:

> It wasn't clear to philosophy, that the impulse behind the cultural ideas it was meant to promote was slowly becoming irrelevant. At the end of one of the most distinguished works on the history of philosophy, published at the end of the nineteenth century ...

—the same work that I've also criticized in a public lecture[18]—

> ... this is defined as the process with which we, and now he quotes this historian of philosophy[19]: *'with ever clearer certainty reflect on those cultural values, whose universal validity is the subject of philosophy itself.'*

Now Schweitzer says to this:

> The author forgot however the most important point: that in earlier times philosophy didn't just commemorate cultural values, but promoted them as active ideas in public thinking, whereas from the second half of the nineteenth century onwards philosophy became more and more a guarded and unproductive asset.

Nobody had noticed where human thinking had ended up. Read some of the reflections that appeared at the turn of the century. Anything done differently as for example was done in my book, later titled

Riddles of Philosophy, was seen as unhistorical. And because at the time the book was titled *World and Life Conceptions in the Nineteenth Century*, a philosopher criticized it on the grounds that there was no mention of Bismarck[20]. There were other similar criticisms of the book, made precisely because it tried to crystallize out of the past those factors that would be active in the future. And what did these observers usually do? They remembered. They commemorated culture as it was. They no longer had any idea of the fact that culture had existed much earlier on.

However, now Albert Schweitzer seems to give up on the future of philosophy. He says it's not really the fault of philosophy that it doesn't play a productive role in modern thinking. This is just the fate of philosophy. The world in general has forgotten how to think and philosophy has forgotten it too. In a certain sense Schweitzer is even quite forgiving, because he could think: even if all the world has forgotten how to think, at least the philosophers could have gone on cultivating it. But Schweitzer thinks it quite natural that the philosophers have, with everybody else, forgotten how to think. So he says: 'The fact that thinking hasn't been able to establish an optimistic, ethical world view and to ground in it those ideals which make up our culture is not due to philosophy, but is just the result of the way thinking has developed.' This was the case in general. 'But philosophy did wrong the world by not admitting to this fact and persisting in the illusion that it was promoting cultural progress.'

Thus, Albert Schweitzer says in razor-sharp criticism, that the philosophers have forgotten how to think along with the rest of the world; but it's not really their fault, it's just a fact. However, the real fault lies in the fact that they've not even noticed it. They should at least have noticed and spoken about it. Schweitzer only reproaches philosophers on the one point.

> In the last resort philosophy is the guide and the guardian of reason in general. Philosophy's duty was therefore to concede that the ideals of ethical reason no longer find their basis in a complete view of the world, but that these ideals now stand alone and will have to assert themselves in the world only through their own inherent strength.

And then he closes the first chapter by saying:

> Philosophy has concerned itself so little with civilization that it didn't even notice how philosophy itself and civilization with it were becoming more and more philistine. In the hour of danger, the watchman, who should have sounded the alarm, was asleep. This is how it came about that we didn't fight for our culture.

Now I ask you not to take Schweitzer's words in the wrong way and say that they are true for German culture but not for England, not for America and least of all of course for France! Schweitzer wrote a large number of books and some of them were written in English: *The Mystery of the Kingdom of God*; then *The Quest of the Historical Jesus*; there is even a third. And he wrote several even in French. This man is really international and is certainly not only speaking about German culture, but about contemporary culture. Therefore, it wouldn't be right if what we saw in Berlin recently would be the attitude we take towards his observations. We were having an anthroposophical meeting and there was one member present who had a dog. Now I have often explained that humans go through repeated earthly lives, reincarnations, but that animals do not, as they have group spirits which are in the same stage, not the single individual animal. This person loved their dog so much that even though they admitted that other animals, even other dogs, don't have repeated earthly lives, *their* dog however did have them, they knew this for certain. There was some discussion about this—discussion can be enlivening, as you know—and you can imagine that this person couldn't be convinced, but that the others were quite sure. This became clear as we sat in the coffee shop afterwards. Another member said how silly it was of the person with the dog to think it would be reincarnated; this is obviously not possible, we can see this from anthroposophy in general. But of course, if it had been their own parrot, that would be different! I don't want you to use this argument in the case of various nationalities, so that you say: this is true of those people that Albert Schweitzer is talking about, their culture is in decline and even their philosophers don't notice it; but our parrot will be reincarnated!

In the second chapter Schweitzer talks about 'circumstances in our economic and intellectual life which inhibit culture' and here too his thinking is remarkably clear. Sometimes he writes something trivial or some remarks which are quite obvious. But then Schweitzer reveals one of the deficits of the modern human being, this uncultured modern person, in that he sees how having lost culture, they have become on the one hand unfree and on the other they are unconcentrated. Now I've read some sentences of Max Rubner to you—they don't exactly show concentrated thinking. Unconcentrated is precisely the right description of the contemporary human being.

Then Schweitzer describes this modern person quite astutely: apart from being unfree and unconcentrated, they are also 'incomplete'. Now just imagine: all these modern people think that they walk around in the world in a state of completeness. But Albert Schweitzer considers that through modern education each person is channelled into a narrow professional life, which only develops their talents in a one-sided manner and lets the rest wither away, so that they become, in effect, incomplete human beings. And also, in this unfree, incomplete and unconcentrated modern person, there exists a certain inhumanity: 'In fact for two generations now, thoughts of a consummate inhumanity are at large among us, in the ugly immediacy of language and with the authority of logical principles. The mentality of society has developed in such a way that it diverts people from humanitarianism. The courtesy of natural sensibility is disappearing.' I just want to remind you of the general assembly[21] we had here, where there was much talk of courtesy!

> Instead we have a kind of behaviour of complete indifference. Acting towards strangers with deliberate aloofness and apathy is regarded not as inner coarseness, but as urbane behaviour. Also our society has ceased to recognize the dignity and value of each individual human being. Some human beings have become for us just human material, human resources. And if now it has become increasingly possible to speak airily of war and conquest, as if they were just moves on a chessboard, then this is because of the general attitude in society at large, which no longer sees the fate of individual human beings, but only regards them as ciphers and objects. As war broke out, the inhumanity

that was already in us, was given free rein. And in the last decades what sheer and coarse brutality with regard to coloured people has found its way into our colonial literature and our parliaments as reasonable argument and has crossed over into public opinion! Twenty years ago, from the rostrum of a parliament on the European continent it was said of deported black people, who had been left to die of hunger and disease, that they 'perished', as if they were speaking of animals.

Now Albert Schweitzer discusses the role of over-organization in the decline of our culture. The over-organization, which prevails everywhere in public life, acts as a cultural inhibitor. These days organizational regulations, laws and provisions are being put in place everywhere. Whatever you do you have to belong to an organization. People accept this without thinking. They act thoughtlessly. They're always organized in some way, so that Schweitzer finds that this 'over-organization' has had a thoroughly constraining effect on culture.

> The terrible truth, that with the advance of history and economic development, culture becomes not easier but more difficult, has never been said. . . . The bankruptcy of national culture, which becomes increasingly obvious from decade to decade, is destroying the modern human being. The demoralization of the individual by the collective is well under way.
>
> An unfree, unconcentrated and incomplete human being, disoriented in their loss of humanity, delegating their intellectual independence and their moral judgement to organized society and trapped in every respect in contemporary cultural attitudes: the shadow human being goes his shadowy way in shadowy times. Philosophy had no understanding of the danger humanity was in and so it could not come to its aid. Philosophy didn't even encourage public debate about what was happening.

In the third chapter Albert Schweitzer says that a real civilization must be grounded in ethics. Earlier world views gave birth to ethical values; but since the middle of the nineteenth century society continued to live with these ethical values without grounding them in a complete world view and they didn't even notice it:

> They lived in the situation born out of an ethical culture without waking up to the fact that it had become unsustainable and without looking at what was developing in and between nations. So, thoughtless as we are,

contemporary humanity came to the conclusion that civilization primarily consisted of scientific, technical and artistic achievements and could well manage without or at least with only a minimum of ethics. This externalized version of civilization was further authorized in public opinion by the fact that well-known figures, whose position and scientific education would lead one to believe they had a certain intellectual competence, supported it. . . . Our sense of reality consists of moving from one fact to the next based either on our passions or on our balance sheets. As we have no clear intention as to what we're trying to accomplish, our activities fall into the category of natural phenomena.

And Schweitzer sees with great clarity that, because they had no creative cultural life, people turned to nationalism.

It was symptomatic of the pathological state of nationalistic realpolitik that it always sought to embellish itself with ideals. The struggle for power became a struggle for rights and for culture. Nations formed egoistic interest groups with each other and presented these as friendships and natural kinship and predated all this to an earlier time, even though history attested more to age-old animosity than to inner affinity.

And in the end, it wasn't enough for nationalism to suspend any aspiration to developing a culture of humanity. It destroyed the whole idea of culture itself by proclaiming 'national culture'.

So you see, Schweitzer has a clear vision in various areas of life. And he finds the words to express this negative aspect of our times. It's quite clear to him how science has affected contemporary life. Since he's quite aware that no one in our time is capable of thinking—I showed you this with the example of Max Rubner—he also knows that science itself has become thoughtless and therefore can't be in a position to lead humanity in a cultural sense.

Today there is no thinking in science since it has become indifferent to thinking. Progressive knowledge goes hand in hand with the most thoughtless world view. It claims to consist just of single statements, as only these can be guaranteed in objective science. Putting the findings into context and evaluating the consequences for a world view is not the task of science. In the past each scientist was also a thinker of importance in the life of the mind of their generation. Our age has arrived at a differentiation between science and thinking. This is why we have perhaps freedom in science but almost no more thinking in science.

Schweitzer sees the negative side extremely clearly and he knows how to express the important point, which is that we must bring spirit back into culture. He knows that culture has excluded the spirit. This morning in the lecture on education[22] I discussed how from what humanity once knew of the soul only the words are left. People still speak of the soul but they don't associate anything real with the word. And it's just the same with the spirit. There is no awareness of spirit; there is only the word. When someone so astutely characterizes the negative side of modern civilization, then—as nobody knows anything of the spirit any more—they can at the most, drawing on certain traditions, say we need the spiritual.

But if they had to say how spirit should be brought back into culture, then it would be like this story that I personally experienced. As a young boy I lived near a village, where one day one of the grandest of the village dignities had his hens stolen. This went to trial and the judge wanted to evaluate how high the punishment should be and therefore wanted to get an idea of what kind of hens they were. And so he asked this village dignitary to describe the hens. 'Yes, your honour, they were lovely hens.' 'But I need to know what kind of hens they were. They were your hens, you must know what kind they were. Describe them in more detail for me, will you?' 'Yes, your honour, they were just lovely hens.' And so it went on. They couldn't get more out of him than: 'They were just lovely hens.'

In the next chapters Albert Schweitzer wants to be more positive and to describe more exactly what he means by a total world view or philosophy. 'What kind of world view would be a thoughtful one, into which cultural ideas and high-mindedness were integrated? Optimistic and ethical.' They were just lovely hens! It would have to be optimistic and ethical. Yes, but what exactly? Just think if an architect was going to build someone a house and wants to know what kind of house the person wants and they only answered: the house has to be stable, weatherproof and a good place to live. Now make a plan for the house on this basis! But it's just the same as when someone says a world view should be optimistic and ethical. If you want to build a house, you have to make a plan and it has to be a practical plan. But

Albert Schweitzer, who is such an astute thinker, doesn't know what to say other than that they were lovely hens. Or that the house should be fine, namely optimistic and ethical.

He does actually expand a little on that, but not much else emerges apart from the lovely hens. For example, he says that as thinking has become unfashionable, nobody can think any more and even the philosophers haven't noticed that there's no longer any thinking, and believe that they can still think. This is why many people turn to mysticism, which works without thinking, which tries to achieve a world view without thinking. Now he says why shouldn't we approach mysticism with thinking? So now the coming world view should be mysticism combined with thinking. But how is this supposed to work? The house should be stable, weatherproof and beautiful and built so that we can live in it. Our world view has to be able to combine mysticism and thinking. But this is just more of the same. Nowhere is there any real substance, not even the tiniest suggestion.

Now how does anthroposophy differ from this kind of cultural critique? As far as the negative aspects are concerned, we can go along with them, but is anthroposophy satisfied with this description of the house: stable, weatherproof, beautiful and built to live comfortably in? No, anthroposophy devises plans for the house, designs in fact a concept for civilization. However, Albert Schweitzer resists this idea and says: 'The great change in the ideals and convictions, that we live in and for, can't be brought about by trying to convince people of better ideas than they themselves have. It will only happen when many people start to think about the meaning of life...' So it's not possible to convince people of better ideas than those they already have! What does Schweitzer think we should do? He exhorts people to engage in serious soul-searching and to develop what's necessary out of themselves, so that nobody else needs to convince them of ideas that they don't already have.

However, it's exactly because people searched their souls for what they already had, that we arrived at the point described at the beginning: 'Our times are characterized by the decline of civilization.' 'There is no reflecting on culture and in fact we've abandoned it altogether.' And so on. And all this has happened—and here

Schweitzer's thinking is astute and right on the mark—because human-ity has neglected to make plans for the house. And now he says that it's not possible for them to absorb anything new, they have to search their own souls. Now you see that it's not only Max Rubner who can't cope with thinking, but even such a terribly clever thinker as Albert Schweitzer isn't capable of moving on from a negative critique of our civilization to recognizing that culture must be enriched by a renewal of spiritual life. Anthroposophy has existed here for the same length of time—since 1900 according to his own report—as Schweitzer has been working on his book. But he hasn't noticed that anthroposophy offers a positive perspective on what he can only negatively criticize: bringing spirit into culture. He even gets a little jocular at the end of the last part:

> It's valuable in itself to think about the meaning of life. If we start to think about this again, then all the ideals of vanity and passion, that have prolif-erated like weeds among the population, will just wither away. How much could be gained, if we all took three minutes each evening and looked up in contemplation to the infinite worlds of the starry skies.

Thus, he means it would be good for people if they took three min-utes each evening and looked up to the heavens! If you say it like that, people certainly wouldn't do it; but look at how it's described in my book, *How to Know Higher Worlds*. It's difficult to understand why he's not able to take the step from the negative to the positive. '... and if, when attending a funeral, we thought about the riddles of life and death instead of idly chatting away as we follow the coffin'.

So you see, if you're only negative, then you have to conclude such a study of cultural decadence as follows:

> Previous thinking aimed at understanding the meaning of life by understand-ing the meaning of the world. But it's possible that we have to leave the ques-tion of the meaning of life aside and try to give our life meaning through our will to live, as it exists in us. Even if the paths leading to our goal are still in shadow, the direction we have to take is clear.

As clear as is the fact that they're lovely hens and as clear as are the plans for the stable, weatherproof, beautiful house. Most modern human beings regard it as clear, when they just describe something and they don't notice how it's really completely unclear.

'Together we have to reflect on the meaning of life; together we have to struggle to find a broad and life-affirming world view, in which the need to act, which we experience as necessary and valuable, can find its justification, orientation, clarification, intensification, moral vindication and strength ...' The house should be beautiful, stable, weatherproof and we should be able to live comfortably in it. The equivalent of this description of the house is that of the world view which should provide our actions with justification etc.! '... And would thus be able to establish and realize definitive cultural ideals in the spirit of true humanitarianism.'

So there we have it. With regard to the negative he shows astute and commendable thinking, but a complete inability to recognize anything positive. For those people who are today worthy of our praise—and Albert Schweitzer is one of the most praiseworthy—this is their situation. This is something anthroposophists should be clearly aware of, so that they recognize those people, who are philosophers in the sense of this sharp-witted Albert Schweitzer, and who, for example, call themselves 'neo-Kantians' and have not only forgotten how to think, but indeed haven't even noticed that they've forgotten. You can't expect such a person to understand anthroposophy. But we should keep a wary eye on these people, who Schweitzer rightly described as the slumbering philosophers of the nineteenth and twentieth century, and on how they speak about anthroposophy. In present times we have to keep our eyes open warily in all directions.

For example one news item reports how little Bergson has held up against Kant[23]. But then they say that the wild speculations of Steiner and his great spiritual tirades hold up even less, when put to the test of Kant's epistemology. Steiner too believes that he can attain a knowledge beyond that of Kant and the Neo-Kantians. In fact, he lags far behind them and, as one can see from his writings, has completely misunderstood some of the crucial points.

This is then broadcast without any further explanation in widely read newspapers. And then someone who thinks in this way—who isn't even able to think as well as Rubner—asserts that you only need to turn to modern science, then you'll know what this so-called knowledge of Steiner's is worth. He calls it 'brain bubbles'.

We have to pay attention to such things and not just let them pass us by. Because this thoughtless science, as Albert Schweitzer calls it, wields power in the world at least for the time being. Many people say that we should be guided by justice and not by power, but then they mistake their own power for justice. I will spare you any more of the nonsense[24] that this author writes, as he then goes into spiritism and how science should examine these phenomena etc.

But when the poor students turn to anthroposophy and absorb these 'brain bubbles', then Max Rubner gives them the following advice: 'It's always very refreshing to start work on a new unploughed field of the brain.' Some fields have been ploughed again and again! So, when the 'brain bubbles' of anthroposophy start to rise up before these poor students and they then start to plough the fields of the brain, then the bubbles will surely be vanquished by the ploughshare. However, in one point they are right: the best minds of our times have characterized modern civilization as decadent and in decline, but insofar as they're part of contemporary cultural life, they are incapable of recognizing the positive aspects. They're stuck in the stage where, when they're supposed to say what the house should be like, instead of taking up a pen or modelling clay, as does anthroposophy, they still just say that the house should be beautiful, stable, weatherproof and made for comfortable living. That's for the house; for a world view they say it should be optimistic, ethical, should provide us with an orientation and so on.

You can see how necessary it is to go a bit further than what is happening in modern civilization. This is why I've given you these episodic observations today. Next Friday we'll speak further about this and not in the sense of the house should be beautiful, stable and weatherproof or the world view should be optimistic, ethical and provide us with an orientation and so on. We will go into real anthroposophy, into the spiritual life that our civilization so badly needs.

A Study of The Century From 1823 to 1923

DORNACH, 6 JULY 1923

T ODAY I want to look at the last century from 1823 until today. From a more external point of view you could see the reason for these observations in the fact that the writer George Sand[25] has set her important novel, *The Journeyman Joiner or the Companion of the Tour of France*, that I won't be discussing here, in 1823, a hundred years ago. For some people it will be possible to find inspiration in this novel, as George Sand has such a great and vivid fantasy, that does more to characterize our times than many a so-called scientific historical study. We could even say that this author has succeeded in creating out of the time around the year 1823—especially in the west of Europe, in France—a vivid background for a momentous novel.

Now I'm not going to go into the contents of the novel, but I'll try to give you the spiritual background behind the state of society at that time. George Sand describes a number of characters, who belong to the petit-bourgeois craftsman class and how the adventures of aristocratic families affect these craftsmen's lives. However, what is described so superbly in this novel is the social life of the artisan class. So allowing for differences in national character, George Sand has depicted the way in which people were confronted with the social circumstances of this era. We can trace it further back, even decades back, especially for France, to when those social conditions existed which Goethe describes in his *Wilhelm Meister*. Always allowing for differences in national culture, we can see as the background of the novel how social conditions are vividly described and how an individual outgrows these circumstances, how an aspect of their personality is captured in the fact of their rising above the social conditions of their time.

As you know the characters in Goethe's *Wilhelm Meister* also rise above the social conditions of their time. In the first half of the nineteenth century some people already grasped the parallels between the social background of George Sand's novel and that of Goethe's *Wilhelm Meister*. Of course, we have to allow for the differences of national character. Goethe's novel is thoroughly cosmopolitan and has nothing specifically national or political. Sand's novel is completely national and thoroughly political. This we have to take as given, when comparing, quite legitimately, the two novels.

Now these conditions, constituting the social background, are characteristic of the whole manner in which the modern human being had, in the last decades of the eighteenth and the first half of the nineteenth century, worked their way from the subterranean to the surface level of human existence. Because today the individual human being stands alone in the social order, people can't easily imagine how things were a century ago. Even those people, who are firmly attached to a profession or to a family, still structure their lives in such a way that they also retain a certain freedom from these relationships and that they have room for a certain individuality.

In this respect there's been a radical change in human development in Europe particularly in the nineteenth century. And the inner soul of human beings with regard to social attachment or non-attachment is quite different in the second half of the nineteenth century from what it was in the first half. In the first half—and we're leaving other countries out of this and are speaking only of Western Europe—human beings looked to be integrated in social relationships. They sought connections with people, who had the same interests as they did, common interests which were a combination of class interests on the one hand and of professional interests on the other. For the rural population which at the time was more bound to the land, we have to include the attachment to the earth. But for those, who in becoming craftsmen outgrew the peasant mentality and freed themselves from their bond with the earth, we have to consider that at that time they were desperately searching for social community. And it's remarkable for this first half of the nineteenth century, for that time we're studying today, that notwithstanding the class and caste connections and the professional links, which provide the adhesive holding such communities together, there was a spiritual, a real spiritual background to their development.

In France, however, everything tends towards the national. If we were looking at the same conditions—which in a certain way we would be justified in doing—in a German setting, then we would have to make it clear from the start that a German apprentice, for instance, would also wander abroad during his journeyman years and would take no notice of political borders when looking for an association such as I've described. But the French character, which is thoroughly nationalistic, only allowed the apprentices to wander within French borders.

However, inside the French border those communities related by class and profession, that people were desperately looking for, could develop and behind them we can see the impact of spiritual impulses working in the human soul. When they travelled from town to town these craftsmen felt themselves to have a kind of spiritual home, as in each location they could find the community to which they belonged. When someone became a member of a community in a certain town, this community was represented all over France. This was a century ago. When the apprentice travelled, he would find this society (guild) in the town where he wanted to work for a while. He didn't need to carry any papers as he had the distinctive signs of the society—a certain handshake or some other sign. When he used this special sign, then the others knew that he belonged to a certain association with branches in all the towns of the country.

Now everywhere such societies—I have to emphasize this—were based on a spiritual impulse and if we want to study these things seriously then we'll find that it's quite difficult to discover just exactly what this impulse was.

In France at that time there were basically two such artisans' societies. The one was the 'Loups Devorants' or 'Loups Garous'. The other was called 'Gavots'. Both of them were organized as I've explained and both had meetings at certain times, which were the same in the various towns. At these meetings they first practised the secret signs and then they had ceremonies in which they spoke in symbols and decorated the hall with symbols. There were ceremonies in which legends were narrated, which traced the societies far back in history. The 'Devorants' or 'Loups Garous'—the English word would have to be 'werewolves'—traced their society back to King Solomon and so they narrated a legend going back to him. With the 'Gavots' the legend with various elaborations went back to the Phrygian master builder, Hiram Abiff. These societies had many differences and if we study the various customs carefully then we can gradually discern the spiritual background, which was well known to the members.

An important difference between the two groups is connected to admitting new members and the fact that in many towns both groups were represented. In various towns there were both Devorants and Gavots. Also, it was a strict custom—and they watched over it carefully—that nobody would be trained in a craft, who didn't go through one of these groups. So, the members of the one association were Devorants, members of the other were Gavots. Each craftsman turned to the respective association when he arrived in town, which, after he had given the prescribed secret signs showing he was one of them, would then find him work in his craft.

Now sometimes it happened that in one town there were many more arrivals than there were workplaces. Now the leaders of the two societies didn't know what to do. So it became a question of whether the Devorants or the Gavots should win and be able to allocate more of these workplaces.

It's typical that then there was fierce enmity between the two societies, just as today there are more or less brutal rivalries between the various leaders of the trade unions, and so they had methods to decide whether the one or the other party would prevail. Often the Devorants wouldn't negotiate, but banded together in the town squares and beat the Gavots up. Then the Gavots proposed that a prize should be awarded for some task and the judges could decide whether the Devorant or the Gavot performed better. This is a significant difference: the Devorants tended to resort to brawling and to external actions to decide the contest in their favour; the Gavots through more spiritual methods. So sometimes the one method prevailed and sometimes the other. This is a difference which reveals the spiritual background of the two societies.

Another revealing difference is to be found in their methods of burying the dead. The Gavots buried their dead by walking silently behind the coffin, which was then lowered silently into the grave. To the left and right of the grave stood the most distinguished members of the society, who then whispered certain secret words to each other over the grave. Then they formed a circle and spoke again in mysterious words.

The Devorants, however, accompanied their dead with remarkably loud voices. If you were standing at a distance while a funeral procession passed by, while it arrived at the grave and while they were throwing earth on the coffin, you could hear a noise, which sounded from afar like the howling of wolves. This was just the way in which the members of this society carried out the funeral ceremony and was completely sincere. They thought that they were harking back to old traditions in which people raised their voices and made powerful and wild sounds, as if they were coming from the world the dead person was entering and spilling over into the physical world.

Here you have evidence that in these societies there were traditions from olden times originating in ancient knowledge. The burial customs of the Devorants paid tribute to old concepts of purgatory, or kamaloka as it is also known. The expression 'loups' or wolves already indicates what lies behind this behaviour. These words or at least the idea behind the words, are used in many esoteric teachings to describe what is at work in the human astral body, when intelligence is absent, when regulation through the brain is absent. What asserts itself in a passionate, emotional manner out of the depths of human nature and in the desire to relate to other people in such a way that we even lust after their blood, that is called in many esoteric teachings the wolf. So, if we want to be honest and clear about these things, we can say that the Devorants thought that, on an occasion such as a funeral, they should behave as if they had left their physical body, including the brain, behind them.

And they celebrated the funeral accordingly. While the Gavot ceremony was quiet and gentle, that of the Devorants was loud and turbulent. It was like an unleashing of the astral world expressing itself in this ceremony. The symbols which played a large part in the ceremony, the structure of the legend, these all show that they brought all these elements of ancient times together in a wild way in their funeral rite.

In contrast it's quite characteristic that the other party gave themselves the name 'Gavots'. This comes from 'gave', which is the name of very small spirits, who come down from the slopes of the Pyrenees below the timberline; they don't show themselves but still come down from the heights of the Pyrenees. They are like little elemental spirits representing the people of the Grail, who used to descend from the heights of the Spanish mountains. The members of the other party, the 'Gavots', saw themselves as being like the little spirits who belong to the host of the knights of the Grail.

While the one party, the Devorants, wanted to express what lives in human astrality, the Gavots wanted to express what was in the 'I' according to the understanding of their times. This means that the difference between the two parties was an expression of the difference between the astral body and the human I. And this is the astonishing thing, extremely interesting, that in the first half of the nineteenth century we have societies which exercise enormous influence within their class and their profession, where it's the custom to belong to the one or the other, and that they have such a spiritual background.

It's just a fact that people want to organize their social relationships according to their class and their profession. Thus, such societies use class and profession as a kind of adhesive. But still such societies of the first half of the nineteenth century would have found it incomprehensible to have mere professional associations such as trade unions. Towards the outside these societies were professional associations, similar to how human beings have an external physical body. But towards the inside they were founded on the soul-spiritual and attached great importance to their secret signs and symbols in which they lived and which guaranteed that the pure character of the society was preserved.

Notice the huge difference between those times and ours. You have to take into account that people learnt very little in school at that time; their intellectual education didn't come from school, where they only just managed to learn to read and write and do a little arithmetic. For the general population other subjects were only later gradually introduced into schools. Even so at that time the general population weren't ignorant. Now the saddest part of our way of looking at history, is that we only ever base it on documents that can be found in the archives of the state or town or whatever. But this isn't at all real live history. We can only find that when we can look into the souls or the minds of the people of the relevant time, the relevant profession or the relevant class.

Those people, who were the leaders of the professions, drew their soul-spiritual nourishment from the meetings of their society. They didn't have an abstract school education. Now it's interesting that as education became increasingly the task of schools it became more and more intellectual and abstract. In all these societies education wasn't intellectual and abstract, but had a more figurative and symbolic character, something which grasped the world in images. When they spoke about the world, they spoke in images and these images came from the societies. And people guarded these images that they received in one or another of the societies carefully, because they knew that in knowing and using the symbols in these closed societies, the will was guided in a certain direction and above all it was guided to attain a certain strength. Whereas abstract education doesn't influence the will at all, the kind of education these people received affected their whole person. In a sense they were each as persons also always representatives of what lived spiritually in their society.

So these societies were very important for the world of that time. And we won't have a social history of the nineteenth century until we include the fact that in such associations spiritual movements were alive, which inspired the craftsmen, those people between the peasants and the nobility, and lived in their souls. Contemporary history doesn't show what lived in their souls because the historians aren't interested in it.

Then suddenly, in the middle of the nineteenth century, ideas appear. Ideas appear in the political parties which developed around the middle of the nineteenth century and all kinds of ideas appear in the works of the politically inspired poets. What kind of ideas are they? Anyone who knows history, real history, knows that these ideas lived in associations and weren't written down. Then certain people started to write everything down and have it printed. This caught on and in the middle of the nineteenth century it became generally accepted. Members would have resisted if this journalistic way of thinking had tried to insinuate itself into their associations. They would soon have shown anyone, who tried to impose it on them, the door! Their whole culture was based on the living human being.

So people who had no feeling for the living human aspect brought this lack into poetry, journalism and into the whole culture that started to take over the world from the middle of the nineteenth century onwards. This flows from underneath up to the top, where it takes on strange forms, which are then incorporated in official history. This kind of history is not real because it has no idea where to find the origins of such things; it just trivializes and makes a caricature of the past. Sometimes there was great depth in the rituals of these old societies, which were then ridiculed by historians. In fact, these societies gave their members a soul connection to the spiritual world in the widest sense.

Now to illustrate this the year 1823 is well chosen, because at this point a number of years have passed since the ideals of equality of the French Revolution. But these spiritual connections had persisted during and after the years of the revolution. People still talked about the ideas of the French Revolution. But how they found their position in life, how they approached other people when they wandered from one town to another, all this was regulated according to the customs prevailing in their societies. People were rooted in social life by being members of the one or the other association.

You have to consider that modern life, which we can legitimately say leads to individual freedom, begins in the fifteenth century, as I've often explained. The old bonds, the old ties don't hold people together any more. The further we go to the west, the less people are held together by these old bonds. The further we go to the east, the greater the role old blood ties play, because the old customs have survived there. As you go west people become more and more isolated and social relationships become more individual. But people sense that they can't yet be completely independent, because complete independence will take two thousand years and we're only in the first millennium after the fifteenth century. However, in the nineteenth century there's been a revolution in this respect. But if we disregard the upper ten thousand, as we like to call them, the nobility or the intellectual nobility, and we look at the mass of the people, then we have to say that they are resisting the process of individualization. Well, those who are in the grip of individualization are also resisting it. The nobility, the clergy, they can hold together, they have bonds. The artisans are being alienated from their bonds and so what they are desperately looking for in these associations are bonds to replace those which don't exist anymore and which they have to create themselves.

So from the fifteenth and sixteenth century onwards, we see craftsmen separating themselves from the peasantry, not able to reach up to the nobility, the clergy or the clerks, but forming these associations, which are held together by a spiritual background. They strive to build up ties among themselves. And it's impressive to see that they don't look for social relationships through their craft—even if it's the craft that forms the setting for it—but they look to the soul-spiritual. So, they can only feel themselves truly human by having on the one hand their craft and on the other, freedom within the craft to follow a world view, when this is an integral part of being human. This is the mark of the turnaround in the nineteenth century, that these spiritual leanings are lost, even though it's preserved in the mumbo jumbo of all kinds of secret societies, which however don't have any connection to the real world. The Freemasons and other secret societies imitate what was cultivated in the craft associations, which were internally held together by spiritual bonds. And if you look at the fact that through the two branches, the Devorants and the Gavots, the members cultivated the astral and the 'I' respectively, then we can recognize this structure of the human being working as impulses in human history.

If we look at the geography, then we see that there were Gavots and Devorants all over France, but that in the northern French towns the Devorants were more numerous and in the southern towns the Gavots. This is connected to the fact that there is a fine difference between the more southern, warmer climate and the northern, colder climate, in that the colder climate favours the development of the human astral nature and the warmer climate that of the human 'I'. This is why when we get into warmer climate zones the difference in the colour of the blood between the arteries and the veins becomes less pronounced, whereas in the north people have a distinct difference between the red and the blue blood vessels. This difference disappears the more you come into warmer climate zones. The less differentiated the colour of the arterial and the venous blood, the more deeply the astral body, and with it the prevailing 'I' configuration, are immersed in their 'I'. The more we get into warm climes, the more 'I' we find. It's interesting that the external geographic conditions are connected to whether human beings tend to have more 'I' or more astral body.

Thus, we see that when we follow history, we can only recognize external historical forces, when we know that in the one group of people the astral is more active and in the other the 'I'. Only if we know the astral being and the 'I'-being can we really follow the driving forces behind history. What's written in the history books nowadays is just as if a person working in a telegraph office but ignorant of the technology, were to write a book on telegraphy, saying: I understand this better than those who have studied it, because I was there. Modern historians are just like this with regard to the facts. But only someone who knows the inner operative forces really has a grasp of historic facts, and these can only be understood through inner knowledge of the human being. And it's the same with geography. Geography shows us that human beings are spread out over the various areas of the earth according to race. The races aren't only different one from the other by their hair colour or the shape of their noses, they are different in the way their etheric, astral and 'I' beings are integrated in the human being. This is all related to the spiritual.

In the times I've been speaking of in this study of a century, even when forming a society of their own free will, human beings acted in accordance with the spiritual impulses at work in the various regions. In northern France they sought more what comes from the astral, in southern France what comes more from the 'I'.

However, if humanity is to become one over the whole of the earth, these disparities have to be mixed with each other again. This is why we see that the longer these societies exist, the more their differences wear away and the members start to mingle with each other. At the end of the eighteenth century, before the French Revolution, we find how with great enthusiasm and emotion people belonged to their societies, how the Gavots were full of ambition to prevail spiritually and the Devorants to win through force. But the whole human being was involved in a worthy manner in being a member of such an association, which takes into account the spiritual impulses at work in the world.

Such things show us how fast human soul constitution can change over time. People are blind if they think they are just the same as their parents. That may possibly be true for the present, although if you know children then you will know that in their souls they're not like their parents were at that age. But if we go back a hundred years, to the time when there was this great turnaround in the middle of the nineteenth century, then we find that there's a huge difference in the configuration of human social relationships in comparison with today.

This reconfiguration of the social entity is real history and not what you find in the archives. There is a simple book[26] by an apprentice carpenter written about 1821, a sort of catechism for the journeyman with all the external details such as how to travel and so on, but you can learn a lot about history from it, if you can see through the outward descriptions to the historic background.

So you see even in the details it is only possible to enliven historical reality through spiritual science. This is why spiritual science is not just an accumulation of knowledge, not just an extension of what is taught in schools today, but can only be compared to waking up in the world, to an awakening. Other sciences—and we can keep this between ourselves—can be compared to someone who pulls their nightcap over both their ears. But anthroposophy should be a real awakening. This is why it also wakes us up with regard to history.

Today in the year 1923, I wanted with these practical observations to make a start on a study of the century which goes back to 1823. George Sand's novel was just a trigger, because of course she doesn't have any idea about the spiritual background. But with a certain instinctive genius, she describes the year 1823 and those times so vividly, that the reader feels motivated to carry the study forward up to the year 1923.

COMMUNITY BUILDING IN CENTRAL EUROPE

DORNACH, 7 JULY 1923

YESTERDAY I attempted a study of the past century by describing how in Western Europe people joined together in associations, which were related on the one hand to their class and on the other to their occupation, and we saw how these associations had a spiritual background. We even had to go as far as the human astral and 'I' beings in order to study the two craft organizations, the 'Devorants' and the 'Gavots'. The essence of these societies, which were more prevalent in Western Europe, where the new civilization was primarily developing, was that people felt themselves to be members of the community with their whole soul-being and that the various secret signs, the symbols, the legends, that I've already talked about, even though they were spiritual in nature, all had links to their lives as craftsmen. The descriptions I gave you yesterday of life a century ago don't hold true for life in the more central parts of Europe. This is why it's understandable that George Sand chose these associations as a background to illustrate certain social problems. We could justifiably say that Goethe tried to do something similar with *Wilhelm Meister*. He wanted to describe how people are connected to other people, to the spiritual and to their profession and how the individual human being develops out of general humanity. Goethe tried to do this in *Wilhelm Meister*. If they'd been a reality for him as they were for George Sand, he would certainly have chosen such associations as a background. He didn't use them, because in those countries where Goethe was at home by dint of his cultural education, they didn't exist as such.

This is the remarkable thing, that since the fifteenth century, when humanity first started to be preoccupied with intellectualism, human problems were regarded very differently in Central Europe than they were in the West. Yesterday I had to describe to you how the individual journeyman wanders around France, how in some town or other he becomes a member of a virtually secret society, how he receives the secret signs and then how, as he continues his wanderings and comes to some other town, he'll find a branch there. He would identify himself and would be accepted into this branch of his society. This is how it was still in 1823 and these guilds deeply influenced the life of the respective crafts and professions.

But we couldn't say the same of Central Europe. For the people of Central Europe we'd have to say that since the fifteenth century their aspiration was to cultivate the human self, the individuality. There wasn't such an intensive relationship between the individual person and their craft or their social class as there was in the West. Therefore people treated their profession as a more external affair. They didn't identify their spiritual life completely with their profession.

In the West their identity and their spiritual symbols were taken from the professions. This wasn't the case in Central Europe. There, spiritual life was separate from professional life and if you inclined towards the spiritual, then your spiritual life was separate from both your profession and your class. So you would live in such a way that if you wanted to devote yourself to the spiritual, you mentally left your professional life behind. This meant that in Central Europe they cultivated those aspects of spiritual life which had nothing to do with professions or social class.

The relationship of the human being to the world was seen without any regard for nations or national context. The focus was on the human being per se. So that if one person, for instance an artisan, wanted to devote themselves to the spiritual life, then they would do so as an individual. They would reflect on the meaning of life as an individual human being. At the beginning of the nineteenth century this person didn't receive the impulse for a spiritual life from an association such as I described yesterday, so in Central Europe spiritual impulses developed in a completely different way.

The individual craftsman who felt the need for self-reflection, a contemplator, would discover what was left of that body of knowledge that used to be alchemy; this has nothing to do with class, nationality or profession. They would also become familiar with what was left of the old astrology. And what they then absorbed of all this, they would consider a valuable and important treasure for their fellow human beings. Then they would wander from place to place. They were always just individuals, no secret signs, just a human being. At first there were strange names for such people. These names emerged in a time when there was a confusion of old and new and anyone who was a bit different was at first viewed with suspicion and called for example a 'Knight of the Golden Spur'. Someone like that had to prove that they had something of importance to say to people before they would respect them. As there were no connections through societies or the like, people who wanted to know who these individuals were had to rely on their own impressions. So if they could gain respect by dint of what they'd learnt, then they had a certain influence. And if someone was well-known in this way, people would talk about their arrival on a certain day.

At first people would find someone like that strange, but after they'd passed through they would think about what they'd said and would wonder how someone could have so much learning in their head and it still be the same size as their own!

The whole way in which they dealt with spiritual life was different, more on an individual level. So it came about that education in the West became much more universal, because it was connected to the professional and class associations. In Central Europe however, there developed a great divide between the educated and the mass of the people who were uneducated. This is part of the great tragedy of Central Europe, the deep divide between those who benefited from the old knowledge, be it astrology or alchemy, and who could then delve more deeply into understanding the human condition, and the rest of the population who were stuck at the level of second-hand ideas, many of them religious.

This was the situation Goethe was faced with. He couldn't describe in his novel *Wilhelm Meister* a situation such as George Sand used in *The Journeyman Joiner*. Goethe had to describe individual people, human individualities and their relationship to the higher worlds and to the lower worlds. In France astral activity is shown in the Devorants and 'I' activity in the Gavots; this permeated both societies. But in Central Europe we have to look at how the individual human being relates on the one hand to the heavens and on the other to the earth.

In an abstract and refined way, Goethe has very nicely brought out what has existed in Central Europe since the fifteenth century as human knowledge and human wisdom in the characters of Makarie on the one hand and the metal-diviner on the other.

Makarie, who is a remarkable figure, appears in Goethe's *Wilhelm Meister*. She is a mature female personality, who because of her weakness as an invalid doesn't completely live in the world; she has, so to speak, raised herself above earthly life and hardly moves about in an earthly manner any more. Everybody reveres her, all the people around her, her family in the narrower and in the broader sense, and because she is independent of all earthly things, she's developed a remarkable cosmic life. And Goethe describes this cosmic life, as if Makarie takes part more in the life of the stars than in the life of the earth, so that all physical considerations have disappeared from her soul and she is completely dedicated to the laws of the cosmos. But the more she dedicates herself to the laws of the cosmos and the less meaning natural laws of the earth have for her, the more the laws of nature are transformed into cosmic moral laws. She becomes a moral authority for all who encounter her. And she doesn't represent some borrowed morality, but a morality, which to someone who's on earth but has liberated themselves from the earthly, seems as if the stars themselves have revealed it. And what Makarie proclaims through her stellar vision, her friend, the astronomer, who is now her disciple in the cosmic worlds, interprets for those around her.

In a very subtle way Goethe has described in the context of a higher social class the situation as we should imagine it for the first third of the nineteenth century in general. We have to imagine that at this time in some, but not many, families there were older women who after a certain age couldn't walk any more, were bedridden, their skin pale and transparent, so that you could see the interesting patterns of the blue veins beneath all over the body, and who seldom spoke. But when they spoke, everybody listened carefully to what they said, as these women proved to be seeresses such as Goethe typified in his Makarie. And in the first third of the nineteenth century we find many groups of wisdom seekers, where people told each other about the one or other seeress, where they were to be found, what prophecies they had made and so on. Such things spread out quite far and were passed from one person to another with a certain poetic flair possible in society then, before there were newspapers. Newspapers have played an enormous part in the destruction of spiritual life.

Goethe depicts such a seeress in the person of Makarie. Then at a certain point in *Wilhelm Meister's Journeyman Years* Makarie is contrasted with the figure of the metal-diviner, the friend of Montanus. The metal-diviner can sense in a similar way what is happening in the depths of the earth, we could say the whole spiritual nature of the earth. She knows the secrets of the earthly metals and how the various metals affect human beings. And Montanus interprets what the metal-diviner experiences, just as the astronomer interprets what is revealed through Makarie.

Thus, Goethe juxtaposes the cosmic seeress with the metal-diviner, who because of her special organization—a somewhat pathological organization—can reveal the secrets of the earth. Goethe shows here that he's not looking for what makes people competent and able to carry out their task on earth in those who live in the cosmos, nor in those who live in the interior of the earth. He sees what makes people competent for earthly life there, where a person knows nothing of both faculties, where they work unconsciously and where there is a kind of balance between them like the arms of a scale.

Goethe doesn't know what's behind this, but he feels—and this comes from his old-world education—how these two extremes of life, of spirit, affect each other and in fact make a person into a proper human being when they're not just acting one-sidedly, but when both sides disappear as specifics and then work together to produce a balance in human nature.

Today we can speak from the standpoint of anthroposophy: here we have the upper human being, the nerve-sense being; here we have the middle, the rhythmic being; here we have the lower the metabolic-limb

human being. In a person such as Makarie the upper being is dominant and not in balance with the lower being, because of a pathological
development of the metabolic-limb being, which has fallen into a kind
of torpor. This torpor is not fatal but renders the person unable to
move around in earthly space, so that the head dominates and then
this person will become a cosmic seer. If the nerve-sense organization
recedes and the metabolic-limb system is highly developed as with the
metal-diviner, then this person lives with the earthly, with the forces and
properties of the metals and minerals of the earth. And in the middle
human being is the balance.

At this point in his social novel *Wilhelm Meister's Journeyman Years*,
Goethe wanted to describe the search for humanity in Central
Europe, how the human being is divided into the cosmic on the one
hand and the earthly on the other, and how true humanity can be
found in the balance between the two.

There was much deliberation about the balance between astrology
above and alchemy down below. Certain figures stand out, such as
Paracelsus or Faust, who travelled from one place to another, astonishing people with their knowledge of these secrets and that human
beings can know so much about themselves. But they were not the
only ones. There were little Paracelsuses and little Fausts everywhere,
who had smaller spheres of influence. What we still have today in the
secrets of dowsing for example, was then common practice. Inci-
dences such as the following happened more than once.

A person with such abilities once arrived in a town and impressed
the people with his knowledge of the upper and lower worlds. And
after he'd greatly impressed them and they'd begun to believe in
his authority, they said to him: 'Master, you have to do something
important for us. We need a well and we want you to tell us where we
should build the well.' So, this person goes around the area with the
inhabitants, sometimes stopping at one spot, then going on again,
but then stopping at a place and saying: 'Here it is! Now we have it!'
And there they built the well.

History doesn't mention things like this, which still went on in the
first third of the nineteenth century, even though they were becoming
increasingly rare. But such things are real. Especially among the lower

classes such things were cultivated and constituted their spiritual life. For them spiritual life was to be found in such events, because they had the innermost urge to understand human life not only symbolically but on a cosmic level. They weren't much interested in how human beings were related to their class and their profession. At that time, they could see all this in their guilds, when they went out with their insignia, when they took part in processions and so on, but this didn't have the deep spiritual meaning that it had in the West. In contrast, here a life more withdrawn from the outer world had a great spiritual significance.

I could almost say that in the West people wanted to understand human soul life through external social forces. In Central Europe they wanted to experience social life as human beings in their own skin. This is what squeezed the spiritual life of Central Europe into a certain stratum of society, so that it couldn't become popular as it was in the West. And it's this too which created the great spiritual tragedy of Central Europe. We're now living in a time when it's important that many people become conscious of these things. Only when we really understand the historical context, can we hope that our chaotic civilization will receive new impulses and that new life will flow into it.

In Central Europe they were already coming down to earth. Particularly Goethe shows this by looking for the balance between the upper and lower human being, and contrasting the two extremes of the metaldiviner and the cosmic seeress. They wanted to put human beings on the earth as active agents; but they also wanted to look up to the cosmic heights on the one hand and down to the earthly, the telluric, on the other, so as to regard people as citizens of the earth. These are the schisms that modern civilization has brought up from the depths.

This is the reason why a work such as Schiller's *On the Aesthetic Education of Man*, which I've often spoken about, where human beings are regarded as simply human, free of any nationality, could only be written in Central Europe. And it was basically taken for granted—even though neither Goethe nor his successors found the solution—that they would also consider how to bring people in general to an understanding of the universality of human nature in this modern way.

This is why in Goethe's *Wilhelm Meister* the so-called educational province plays a large part. Human education becomes a problem, a problem that couldn't be solved at that time, but only in the present day, where we have access to anthroposophical knowledge of the human being.

In the West people had in a way gone beyond their own skin. They were tentatively searching for a way of connecting to other people. How can we show ourselves to another person? How can we grasp their hand? How can we speak so that they understand us? The sign, the handshake and the word, as they were used in an extravagant manner in Freemasonry, these were what had an enlivening, invigorating effect in the West up until the last third of the nineteenth century. In Central Europe they didn't appreciate such symbolism, but they did strive to make sense of the riddle of the human being in general.

It's interesting to compare this with Eastern Europe. There, up to the end of the first third of the nineteenth century and later, human beings came from the inside and didn't quite reach their skin. They remained in a soul state, which didn't quite lift them out of the divine, didn't drive them forward to the human condition. So I could say, that whereas in the West the attitude developed that the world is the world—at best they were thinking about social Utopias—the world is as it is and we have to live in it; we need social institutions in order to live in it, or at least we have to view those we have as if they were splendid institutions. But in Central Europe they demanded that human beings first become human; they have to work themselves up to being human, only then can they discover the earth. In the East they were convinced that both these ideals were wrong. Just the idea that human beings have to work their way up to being human is to them misleading because then they would have to leave paradise. And in reality, people should regard that piece of the earth that they live on as paradise, otherwise life becomes impossible. We should return to what is more unconscious in us instead of going out too strongly into life.

This is why in Eastern Europe there has always been a certain tolerance towards the West and towards Central Europe, a certain benevolence born of human kindness; but those regions where they valued a more external way of being human as in the West, or where they valued more the individual human being as in Central Europe, constituted for the East a kind of falling away from the divine human being. And then as the tendency developed in the East to study the rest of Europe—we can observe this in Russia very clearly—we can see that, as people don't want to come out of themselves, even the best can only achieve a certain tolerance, but not a real inner understanding of the rest of the world. Russians if they are real Russians, can't come as far forward as their own skin; they stay stuck deeply within themselves. It's much too earthly for them to come forward as far as the skin; they have to stay more deeply inside themselves.

You see this was the soul mood that Dostoyevsky had to an extremely high degree. And as he's very representative for Eastern Europeans, it's always interesting to hear what Dostoyevsky has to say to the people of the West.

In the latest issue of the journal *Knowledge and Life*, which has just appeared[27], they have published letters which Dostoyevsky wrote to Apollon Maikov in 1868. But if travelling had been as commonplace in the first third of the nineteenth century, you could just as well have read letters dating back to then.

Some of you sitting here today will have to excuse me for reading parts of these letters, but it's Dostoyevsky speaking and not me. I'm just interested in letting Dostoyevsky speak. Somehow, he ended up in Geneva and now all you Genevans and people from the area have to excuse me for reading parts of a letter he wrote in 1868.

> In Geneva we suffered most from material discomforts and from the cold. If you only knew how stupid, dull-minded, insignificant and wild these people are! It isn't enough just to visit the place as a tourist. No, just try to live here for a while! But I can't tell you all of my impressions now; there are just too many. The bourgeois life in this republic has developed to the non plus ultra. In government, in all of Switzerland—nothing but parties, incessant arguments, pauperism, in everything an appalling mediocrity. The local worker isn't worth the little finger of one of ours; it's ridiculous just to watch and listen to them. Manners are raucous; oh, if you only knew what people here regard as good or bad. Little education, drunkenness, thievery, fraud which is even lawful here. They do have some good sides though, which make them much preferable to the Germans.

Now I have to excuse myself to the other side!

> In Germany what astonishes me the most is how stupid people are; they're unbelievably ignorant, immeasurably stupid. Even our Nikolai Nikolayevich Strakhov[28], a man of great intellect, doesn't want to see the truth. He says: 'The Germans are clever, they invented gunpowder. But this was just due to the way they live.'

He means that the fact they invented gunpowder doesn't in any way ameliorate their terrible stupidity.

> …In Switzerland there is enough forest, in the mountains there is more forest left than in the other European countries, although it's declining terribly every year. Now imagine this: for five months of the year it's terribly cold here and then there's an awfully cold north-east wind as well. And for three months the winter is almost the same as ours. Everybody shivers in the cold, the padded, flannel clothes are never taken off (and there are no steam baths here, so you can imagine the dirt they're accustomed to), nobody has proper winter clothes (flannel alone isn't enough for such a winter), they wear the same ones as in summer, and they haven't even got the sense to winterproof their apartments! What difference does an open fireplace with coal or wood make even if you heat all day? Heating all day costs 2 francs a day. And so much forest is destroyed unnecessarily, because we don't even get warm. What do you think? If they just had double glazing, then we could at least live with the fireplaces without even installing ovens. And we could save the woods. In 25 years, there'll be no forest left at all. They really live like savages! But they can certainly put up with a lot. In my room when it's permanently heated it's +5 degrees Celsius. I was sitting there in my coat, money was supposed to arrive, I had to pawn some valuables and all the while thinking about the plot of my novel. Is that a good life? It's said this year in Florence it went down to -10 degrees. In Montpelier it was -15 degrees. Here in Geneva it only went down to -8 degrees, but it's all the same when the water in your room freezes. I just moved and now I have nice rooms; one of them is always cold but the other is warm, about +10 or +11 degrees Celsius and so I can go on living.

And so he goes on.

So you see, the Central and Western Europeans don't get off lightly in the portrayals of this most excellent of Russians. And we have to ascribe this to the fact that they don't have the possibility of going out even as far as their skin. There is this closed system, which can't harmonize with the environment, but demands that everything else adapts to it.

From the perspective of the history of the time, it's very interesting to read these letters, which have just been published. That's why I chose them and not those from the first third of the nineteenth century, for our study of the century, because in Russia these themes only emerged later, although they were always present below the surface. In this case, we can characterize the time a hundred years ago by looking at the facts of a later time. And we even find things we'd be very surprised at in the West. Now if you want to compare descriptions by Western or Central Europeans, you will find the following passage from a letter from the same date—1 March 1868—interesting. We can see how people can view the world from various points of view.

'As for our courts, having read much, I've formed the following opinion about them: the moral being of our judges'—meaning those in Russia—

> and above all of our juries is infinitely higher than in Europe. They regard criminals as Christians. Even the Russian traitors who live abroad will admit to this. But one thing seems unresolved; I think that in this humanitarian relationship with criminals there is a certain liberality learnt from and dependant on books. You can sometimes see this. By the way, being so far from home, I could be wrong. However, in this respect our essential nature is infinitely more elevated than that of the European.

Here you see that his views on the courts are given from a different perspective than you would usually hear in Western Europe.

I'd like to emphasize two points from the lectures yesterday and today. Firstly, it's absurd to believe that we can use present-day standards to judge the conditions of even as recently as a century ago; we have to respond with care to the circumstances of the past, if we want to develop an opinion that does justice to them. But even with regard to our contemporaries, we have to find a certain generosity in our opinions of them. This is what we have to find nowadays: a way of disregarding the national point of view and discovering that of the citizen of the earth.

But this can only develop out of a deeper knowledge of humanity. The world couldn't achieve this deeper knowledge before the advent of anthroposophy. And we could say that if we really study what was happening in Europe a century ago, we can see that there is a longing for this deeper knowledge of humanity. But with what they knew at the time about nature, it wasn't possible to achieve this deeper knowledge in the modern sense. Then natural science overwhelmed everything in the second half of the nineteenth century; and now we have to search for what the best minds in Europe longed for and which was submerged for a while, so that now we must search for it again with a higher spiritual knowledge.

Only this will give humanity the strength, which can lead to the rise of civilization out of its decline. It's really grim that so little history, so little geography is cultivated in the sense mentioned above, that things have become so bound to outward appearances. The important thing is that we look for the spiritual in history and in a geographical sense all over the earth. Especially history and geography have to go through a metamorphosis in a spiritual sense.

This is exactly what Goethe's 'educational province' in his novel *Wilhelm Meister* did not yet have, even though the longing for it was there in his characters. And so much of the longings of that time are now erupting in our own times. Humanity has to wake up to what was once dreamed of with such yearning, so that the dreams of that time can now become reality through the power of spiritual knowledge. Humanity needs this reality for the future of civilization.

European Culture and its Relationship to The Latin Language

GREEK AND ROMAN MYSTERIES

DORNACH, 8 JULY 1923

From the two lectures yesterday and the day before, you'll have seen that from an anthroposophic point of view we have to recognize how important it is to address in the proper manner what was happening in Europe in the course of the nineteenth century. We were able to connect the phenomena we looked at with what has proved to be the real feature of modern times, which from the middle of the fifteenth century onwards we can count as the underlying characteristic of the spiritual and historical development of Europe.

Now taking those two lectures as the basis, today I'd like to open up our sight and timelines for a larger perspective.

We have to be clear that on the one hand European development in the nineteenth century saw the rise of materialism. And I count as materialism everything that can refer only to material phenomena, when explaining anything about the world; that sees no necessity to turn to the spiritual, when dealing with all that sustains human beings in the world or that guides their development. And on the other hand, in addition to materialism, we have to take into account the rise of intellectualism or rationalism, the view that only accepts what it perceives as logical concepts.

You mustn't assume that because I speak about a logical way of thinking, there must be another illogical or even an anti-logical counterpart. This is not what I mean, of course. For reality, however, logic is similar to what the skeleton is for the human being: logic is always the dead part. This is why the mere logic of reason, that human beings have struggled with so ingeniously, promotes a materialism related only to dead substance.

Now today only studying the true reasons for the rise of materialism on the one hand and rationalism on the other, with no illusions, can help advance human civilization. So today we must go back a little further in time in order to give some background to what we talked about yesterday and the day before.

I've often pointed out what a deep rift there is between what Greek culture once was—that culture which was at least partly expressed in the Greek language—and what gradually developed to the west of it in the Latin language. I've also often mentioned the view of Hermann Grimm, who says that we modern people can still understand the Romans, because basically we have the same concepts as they had; but the Greeks seem to him like the inhabitants of fairyland. I've written about this in more detail in the issue of *The Goetheanum* that has just appeared[29].

Now we have to be clear that Eastern Europe, which I also tried to describe yesterday—perhaps rather controversially for some of those present today—went through a wave of civilization strongly influenced in later ages by the Greeks. In the east of Europe, we encounter late blossoms of Greek sensibility. In Western and Central Europe however, Latin culture spread intensively. And the differences that I described to you in the last two lectures are basically the result of what was a continuing Greek influence in the East and a Roman one in the West.

Don't forget that the West was in a much better position to digest Roman culture than was Eastern Europe—the West absorbed the Latin language for example. Latin had a pathological effect on Central Europe. Only if we can clearly perceive this phenomenon, the final effects of which are currently playing out most dramatically, can we get our bearings in the present cultural situation.

Let us look at the situation first from a Central European perspective. I'd like to draw your attention to what Fritz Mauthner contended from the language side, a linguistic point of view. Mauthner intended to write not so much a critique of reason, basically a critique of concepts, like Kant, but more a critique of language. He thought he'd discovered that when people spoke about higher things, they were really only speaking in words, and that they didn't notice they were only speaking in words. Furthermore, if we study how people use words such as God, spirit, soul, goodness and so on, then we see that people believe that in using these words they have something real, but in reality they're only using words without indicating anything.

Now I've already pointed out that this whole thinking of Mauthner's doesn't apply when we're dealing with natural objects, because in that case people can differentiate very well between the word and the thing. At least I've never had the experience that someone going riding would try to mount the word 'horse' instead of getting on a real horse!

But it's a different matter when we're dealing with the soul or with an ethical or moral question, and this seems to vindicate Mauthner. As regards the soul there are words handed down from the past that people repeat, but the insights connected to them haven't been transmitted. They're using words like soul or spirit, but they don't have any insight into what they mean. Mauthner noticed this on the soul level and thought he could generalize. In the case of the soul or of the ethical-moral realm, moral impulses, for example, have gradually lost their substance and only exist as commandments or even laws from the outside.

Thus for much of our vocabulary real insight into the word has been lost. This is why it's so arduous trying to find an expression for the most important faculties of the human soul: thinking, feeling and willing. For thinking, feeling and willing are things that everybody talks about without having any real idea what they are. The question is, can we discover what's behind the words?

We have to be clear that for many centuries the kind of education which leads ultimately to the life of the spirit was communicated in the Latin language. And the Latin language became, not just as an external description but in a real inner sense, a dead language. The Latin language, that people had to learn in the Middle Ages if they wanted access to higher education, was becoming more and more a mechanism per se. A logical mechanism per se.

You can trace this process if you look at history in the way we did for the nineteenth century yesterday and the day before. If we look at human life from the inside then we see that in the fourth century CE the Latin language gradually ceased being experienced internally; it no longer expresses the logos, but only the sheaths of the logos. It survives in the Italian or the French language, which assimilated a lot of Latin. So they absorbed too some of the death process of the Latin language, but they also assimilated what emanated from the various peoples who moved from east to west and settled in the west. In Italian and in French this other aspect lives on not only in the words, but also in the structure of the language and in the dramatic aspect. However, pure Latin has petrified, the living experiences have disappeared, and in its petrification, it has become the dominant scientific language. And it's precisely the language that we have to study if we want to understand why the mediaeval world view took on the form that it did.

Consider the fact that people were forced into this language as children. They didn't go through a process of forming the language out of their own experiences, rather the language was poured into them as a ready-made instrument and, from the way in which the words were connected grammatically, they learnt logic. Logic became something that was poured into them from outside.

The relationship of the human soul to intellectual education became looser and looser and people couldn't move enthusiastically from their own experiences into education, but were absorbed into a foreign element of education, the petrified Latin element. This then spread out in the soul and pushed what people had already experienced aside or more deeply back into them, into a soul region where they didn't need logic.

Just think of how things were in the Middle Ages and how they were when we were young, if you're as old as me. Then if we said something in our mother tongue and someone in the group didn't understand it, we quickly translated it into Latin and everything was clear. But it became cold and sober. It became logical. If something was expressed in a Latin grammatical case, then you understood how strictly and precisely it was meant.

During the centuries of the Middle Ages they always did this. In their spoken language people allowed themselves the greatest sloppiness, because they associated precision or accuracy with thinking in Latin, which was foreign to them. And because it was foreign and human beings can only reach the spirit through the soul, the Latin language petrified to such an extent that you couldn't use a word if you didn't have the object available in the physical world of the senses. In the case of the horse it didn't work if you only had the word for it, because then you couldn't have ridden it. But for all supersensible phenomena, the content drained slowly out of the words and people were left with the empty shells. And then later as their mother tongue developed, they just translated the word into it. Thus they didn't convey the experience. By putting 'anima' and 'soul' together, whereby 'anima' had lost all real substance, 'soul' also lost all real substance. And so it came about that the Latin language was only suitable for use with the external sense world.

There you have from a linguistic point of view one of the reasons why theology in the Middle Ages said: through science we can only understand external things and at the most the connections between them, but we have to leave the supersensible to faith. If they had developed the strength to speak the whole truth, they would have said: the human being can only perceive what can be expressed in Latin and must leave the rest to a faith, that is inexpressible and can only be felt.

You see in a sense this is the truth and the rest is illusion. The truth is that over the centuries the prevailing view was that only what can be expressed in the Latin language is scientifically true.

Then in the eighteenth century the pretension of the national language arose. Now at that time the various regions of Europe had completely different relationships to their national language. Where Latin still held sway, the vernacular could find its way into education more easily. Hence, we have the situation in Western Europe that we talked about the day before yesterday, that social life, social bonds, as I called them, developed in a popular way, so that everyone could take part; this is because, in the West as national feeling arose, it was related to Latin.

In Central Europe this was completely impossible, because the national languages had no Latin influence. They were very different from Latin. At the top however were the elite, who had to learn Latin to gain access to education. Here the difference was enormous and here is the origin of the whole tragedy of Central Europe that I talked about yesterday. This is the tragedy taking place between the mass of the people, who didn't learn Latin and therefore had no science—for science was always spoken of in Latin—and those who studied science, who switched over for the duration of their science studies. In normal life, when they ate and drank in the company of their compatriots, they were uneducated people, because they were speaking languages containing no education. But when they were scientists, then they were different; they put on their inner cap and gown. This meant that an educated person was basically someone divided in themselves.

This affected the intellectual life of Central Europe profoundly. For a variety of reasons, that we will talk about later, the vernacular contained only what we said yesterday was on the one hand an astro-logical element and on the other hand an alchemistic element. These live in the national languages, which had an inherent spirituality. In Europe the vernacular languages had no materialism. Materialism was forced onto them from the materialism of the Latin language, which as it ceased to be the language of the educated still left behind the basic attitudes it had nurtured in that time. So the Central Euro-pean languages couldn't find a balance with what had been estab-lished through the Latin language as education.

This is an extremely serious matter. We can observe this situa-tion up to the present day. I'll show you a practical example of how strongly we can see it today. In various universities you can study economics as it is called. This field of study has developed out of legal concepts and these are wholly the offspring of Latin culture. To think legally means to think in Latin, even today. Unfortunately these economic concepts bring us back to 'things'. Just as you can't ride the word 'horse', so you can't eat mere economic concepts. You can't keep house with them. As science has developed out of Latin culture—most people aren't aware of this—so current economic science has no real substance. Economics as it's taught today only understands what has nothing to do with reality, because it originated with Latin, failed to establish a connection with contemporary reality and only spins everything out from ideas.

We could say that especially in the case of economics there is a contradiction. I spoke yesterday about those people in Central Europe who were called 'contemplators'—they came from the folk traditions and had therefore the old astrology and alchemy. Contemplator means those who contemplate. People who carried Latin over into economic studies were not contemplators. They were spinners. I mean that seriously! The whole science of economics has been spun out of a mere logical net, which is what has become of the Latin language.

Last autumn I gave a course on the world economy[30]. This was about the real thing and not just the empty word. During this it became increasingly clear that when we speak about the realities of economic life, students of economics can't bring this together with what they learn, with what is just words. It doesn't fit together. Now someone could say, then we should hold a parallel course, that brings the conceptual empty shell that is modern economics, into line with what we learn from reality. But that would mean we should explain the fruitfulness of an orange on the basis of the discarded orange skin; that's just not possible. If we really want to gain knowledge from reality, then we can't just study the empty shell. If we are to understand reality, then we must work anew from the original substance.

In a general education which is not permeated by Latin, but still includes—in a form no longer appropriate for the times—the old science of the heavens and of the earth, astrology and alchemy, there developed the following notion: just as science is what can be said in Latin, so is all that cannot be said in Latin, but only in the vernacular, superstition. This is not explicit because people like to pretty things up. But our whole education is saturated on the one hand with the belief that science is all that can be put into Latin, and on the other hand superstition is all that cannot be put into Latin, but has to be expressed in the vernacular.

This is a phenomenon that was much less widespread in the West, but was an awful tragedy in Central Europe. Then again much less widespread in the East. Firstly, in the East they had allowed Greek, which was much more permeated with the juice of reality, to flow into their culture. Secondly, they didn't take the terrible struggle between their ethnic vitality and petrified Latin culture so much to heart. The people of the East just looked on and said: it's only people who've fallen out of paradise who get caught up in struggles like that. Here in the East we're still in paradise. It only looks as if we've fallen down, we're inner human beings!

So you see we have to go into this if we are to understand the terrible rift that exists today between those people who live in what has been built in the Latin style, and those, who as homeless souls, a description I used here just a short while ago[31], now seek the way to the spirit out of the elemental depths of their own being. People are confronted with the tremendous authority of what is a branch of Latin culture. This respect for Latin culture is behind the contemporary belief in the authority of science.

Just think what it meant over the centuries, when a farmer's son went to the monastery school and had to learn Latin. In the holidays he came home and could speak Latin. Nobody understood anything of what he'd learnt, but they all accepted that they shouldn't and couldn't understand what led to science, to knowledge. That they knew. The farmer's boy who went to the monastery school spoke the language of knowledge, and the other farmers' boys, who worked in the fields, had an enormous respect.

We have respect not for what we know but for what we can't know. This respect for what we can't know is consolidated by the fact that we don't even make a claim to it. This perpetuates itself and takes on forms that we can only understand if we have the will to follow the spiritual paths of humanity. The farmer's boy in the twelfth, thirteenth century, who helped with the ploughing and with other tasks, knew: we can't know anything, we'll never be able to know anything, because only those people can know things who've learnt Latin. That's what the farmer's boy would have said then. This continues under the surface and a few centuries later a scientist gives a speech to the enlightened naturalists' conference, the highlight of which is the same as the farmer's boy said of the monastery school-boy: we cannot know—ignorabimus! If we had a feeling for it, we could go back centuries and find the origins of this statement of Du Bois-Reymond's in what the farmer's boy who hadn't learnt Latin said to the boy who had.

Now a dead language such as Latin, which has become petrified, has the tendency to deaden the words too. However, what is dead in the world is matter. So, in those regions where it was particularly dominant, the Latin language had the tendency to push things towards the dead, that is to say towards the material. As I've mentioned before[32], originally people knew very well what the transubstantiation of bread and wine into the body and blood of Christ meant. They knew this from living experience. The people could have known this too, but the alchemy of the people, not being in the Latin language, counted as superstition. The Latin language however couldn't keep hold of the spiritual. This is how the trivial belief arose about what we imagine is the material aspect of the bread and the wine, which had to be transformed; also all the discussions about the teachings of the Last Supper, which only showed that those taking part in the discussion had absorbed these teachings in the Latin language. But the words had become so petrified that people could no longer understand the living, just as the anatomists of today can't understand the living human being from studying corpses.

Not to have the influence of Latin in its language was a terrible tragedy for Central Europe. The language of Central Europe needed to be able to grow into the living spirit. But thinking was a dead thing, because it was dependent on Latin. Concepts couldn't find words and words couldn't find concepts.

For example, the word 'soul' could have found its living equivalent as did the word 'psyche' in ancient Greece. But in the meantime, there was Latin culture, which knew nothing of living reality and even killed off the living reality that still existed in the vernacular. This is why it's so important today to look at the deep rift that had developed between Greek and Roman culture. And this deep rift is very much in evidence when we study the mysteries.

If we look at Greece first, we have the Eleusinian mysteries, which were the most popular. They were the mysteries that most popularized the spiritual path. The people who were initiated into the Eleusinian mysteries were the 'telestes'. Let us look at what is meant by the name 'Eleusis' and the word 'telestes'.

Eleusis is just the linguistic transformation of the word Elosis, which means the place of the human beings of the future, those who wish to bear the future within themselves. Eleusis means what is coming. And the telestes, or the Eleusinian initiates, are the coming people. This shows that these people were aware that they were incomplete, imperfect, and that they had to become the coming people, who bear the future within themselves. Telos anticipates the future and what will only gradually manifest in the future. In the Eleusinian mysteries, that place of the people of the future, the imperfect human being was transformed into the perfect one and became a telest.

The whole meaning of these initiations broke down when the mysteries were transferred to Rome. In Greece the whole initiation pointed towards the future, to the end of the earth. Human beings should develop a strong inner impulse, so that they could find the right way after the end of the earth. Then you were a telest, who would go on to develop after the end of the earth in the right way.

But when this was brought over into Roman culture the expression 'telest' became the initiate, initium, which means the beginning. So, the goal was relocated from the end of the earth to the beginning. The telestes became the initiates. Those who were initiated into the secrets of the future became those who knew about the past. The Promethean seekers became Epimethean: those who seek knowledge of the past. However only abstract knowledge can remain of the past; if we want to develop into the future, we need a living knowledge full of willpower. The will has to develop accordingly. The past is past. We can certainly develop higher knowledge by going back to the initium, the past, but it's still only knowledge and becomes more and more abstract.

Thus, the impulse to abstract, to petrify, gained pace from the fourth century CE and found its way more and more into the Latin language. People wanted to return to the past, where ideas were connected to life, because they knew that it was no longer the case, that now if they reached out for ideas, they ended up in a kind of petrified speech. In Greece being initiated meant receiving a higher life into your soul. In Roman culture being initiated meant abandoning all higher life for the duration of your earthly life and at most thinking about it as follows: in the beginning of the earth, we human beings had a higher life, but we've fallen away from that now and we can't be active like that anymore; at most we can know something of this higher knowledge.

These are the difficulties we're faced with today. When we form the word 'initiation' for instance, *Einweihung* in German, it contains the verb *'weihen'*, which indicates quite literally 'submerging under water', leaving the sharp contours of physical life behind you and immersing yourself in the elusive watery element of the world, so that your soul moves in the weaving, living, flowing spiritual dimension. To initiate someone is to lead them into the moving, fluctuating, fluid world of life itself. Now they had to translate this and they translated it into its opposite: into initiation, meaning beginning.

It's important to know that such contradictions, such difficulties exist in our modern civilization; we have to be clear about these spearheads, as I'd like to call them, that can do us so much harm. Only then can there develop what will help us to make real progress.

Of course I don't want to hold a tirade against the learning of Latin. Just the opposite: I'd like people to learn more Latin, so that they can get a feeling for the fact that with Latin you can only describe dead things. Latin has its rightful place in the anatomy lesson in the dissecting room, but if we want to study not what is dead but what is living, then we have to turn to the living elements of the language. We can't shape the future with some kind of abstract intention, but only with a vision free of all illusion, which can create from the dead the life of the spirit. And we're living in a moment of time, when this is all becoming very acute in the life of the spirit. We're living in tremendously important times.

I don't know how many of you took seriously what I wrote in the last few issues of *The Goetheanum*, namely that twenty, fifteen, ten years ago you could quote someone like Hermann Grimm just like a contemporary. Today he belongs to the past and we can only speak of him as belonging to the past. I meant what I said in these four articles touching on Grimm very seriously[33]. As you know I used to like to quote Hermann Grimm, but in quite a different manner than I quote him now. I used to quote him where it was possible to show a spirit directed towards the future. Today he belongs to the past, to history, and we can quote this man, who until recently was such a contemporary presence, only when it's a question of illustrating an aspect of ancient Greek or Roman civilization.

But I have to admit that this passage of time, which becomes the past remarkably quickly, demands something else of us. And we sleep through much of it! This gentle sleepwalking is something we are much given to today.

However, anthroposophy is knowledge which we don't just gather as ideas, but which is supposed to wake us up. This is why so many of my lectures are meant to wake people up.

THE GNOSTIC FOUNDATIONS OF PRE-CHRISTIANITY. IMAGINATION OF EUROPE

DORNACH, 15 JULY 1923

IN a time when humanity is faced with great questions and momentous decisions, we have to raise our understanding of contemporary phenomena to the spiritual level. After all the spiritual is not an abstraction, but something which both transcends and affects the physical. Whoever only perceives the physical plane, even if they allow that the physical is permeated with spirit, is only observing a fraction of the world in which human beings think and act. For a few centuries this was justified up to a point. But for the present and the near future this justification has ceased to exist. And so today I want to begin to look at contemporary events in their direct connection to events in the spiritual world and their effects on the physical plane.

Before we can go into this however, we must consider what spiritual impulses affected human development and led us to this moment in history. For many centuries Western civilization and all that grew out of it was defined on the basis of just a fragment of world development. This was quite legitimate. It was legitimate that in times when the Bible with the Old Testament was the ultimate authority, people traced their origins back to that moment in world evolution, when Jehovah created human beings.

In earlier times human beings regarded this intervention of Jehovah as a much later occurrence and not one that they would look back at as the definitive moment. In these earlier times they viewed the creation of the world by Yahweh or Jehovah described in the Old Testament as being preceded by an older phase of development, which was much more spiritual than what people usually imagined in the context of the Bible. For them the moment captured in the Bible, the creation of human beings by Jehovah, only came later, and was preceded by a whole other phase, whereby Jehovah himself was described as a being who only intervened in world development quite late in comparison with other beings.

When they reflected on the initial stages of world evolution, they looked back to Greece and to a primordial being, who was seen as the true creator of the world, the demiurgus or demiurge. To understand this being you would need a much higher level of spiritual cognition than is necessary to understand the Old Testament. The demiurge was presented as a being, dwelling in spheres of exalted spirituality, where there was no thought of a material existence leading to the kind of humanity, which would be created by the Jehovah of the Bible.

The demiurge is a sublime being, a creator of worlds, whose power of creation consists essentially of bringing forth, so to speak, spiritual beings. The beings produced by the demiurge were progressively lower and lower—the expression isn't really appropriate, but we don't have anything else. However, they were still far from being subjected to earthly birth and death.

In Greece they alluded to this by speaking of aeons and differentiated between aeons of the first kind, aeons of the second kind and so on (see diagram). These aeons were the beings emanating from the demiurge. Then in this series of aeons there was a relatively minor being, a minor aeon, Jehovah. And now we come to what in the first Christian centuries the so-called Gnostics offered as a renewal of the contents of the Bible, but where there is always a gap in their understanding: Yahweh or Jehovah united himself with matter. And from this union humanity was born.

Thus, according to their thinking in the first Christian centuries, the act of creation of Yahweh or Jehovah, who was himself a lowly descendant of the sublime aeons right up to the demiurge, consisted of uniting himself with matter and bringing forth humanity.

All that has its basis in the world of the senses, but effectively rises above it—in earlier times humanity understood this, later they no longer did—is summarized in the expression 'pleroma' (see diagram, over).

Demiurg

Aeonen 1

Aeonen 2

Jehova ·········· Materie

Mensch

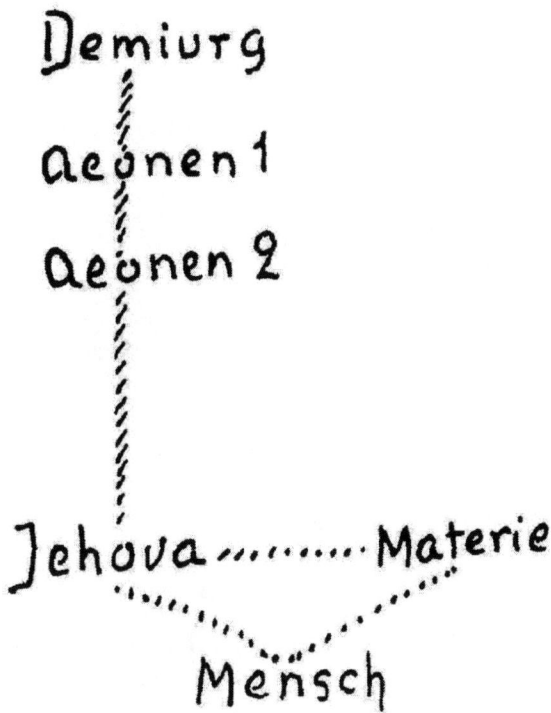

(Demiurg = demiurge; Aeonen = aeon; Jehova = Jehovah; Materie = matter; Mensch = humanity)

Pleroma is therefore a world which transcends the world of the physical and is populated by individualized beings. Virtually on the lowest level of this pleroma world appears the human being, brought to life by Yahweh or Jehovah. On the lowest level of this pleroma a being emerges who lives not in just a single person, nor in one people, but in the whole of humanity, and who remembers our ancestry in the pleroma from the demiurge and strives to regain this spirituality. This is the being Achamoth, who to the Greeks was the personification of the striving of humanity towards the spiritual. So, through Achamoth we have a quest for the spiritual (red arrow).

Now this world imagination is joined by another one: the demiurge has answered the quest of the Achamoth and has sent down one of the early aeons, who then united with the human being, Jesus of Nazareth, so that the striving of the Achamoth would be

Pleroma { Demiurg
          Aeonen 1
          Aeonen 2

Jehova .... Materie ....Achamoth

(grün) (rot)

Mensch

Jesus

(grün = green; rot = red)

fulfilled. Thus, in the human being Jesus there lives a being from the aeon evolution, who is spiritually much higher than Yahweh or Jehovah (green arrow).

Among people in the first centuries of Christianity, who had this imagination—and there were many who looked up to the Mystery of Golgotha honestly and fervently—the idea developed that a great mystery surrounded the human being Jesus because of the primordial and ancient holy aeon, which dwelled within him.

People tried to fathom this mystery in various ways. Today it's not really meaningful to reflect on the various forms in which people in the earliest Christian centuries, in Greece and then in Asia Minor and farther on, imagined how this aeon-being lived in the human being Jesus. This is because the ideas, with which people tried to approach such a mystery, have all long disappeared from our thinking. In our thinking now there exists only what surrounds us in the sensory world, what is connected to us between birth and death; at the most a person might extrapolate what they see around them from birth until death onto what could spiritually lie behind this physical-natural world. The direct and intimate relationship that human souls once had to the pleroma and which they spoke of as their relationship to the spiritual world, just as today people speak about their relationship to trees and shrubs, clouds and waves, all that existed then in their imaginations as images of the connection between humans and the spiritual world, which was to them more interesting than the physical world. All that has disappeared. This direct relationship no longer exists. And we can say: the latest centuries in which you could find such ideas in the civilization from which European or occidental civilization has evolved, were the first, second, third and a large part of the fourth century CE. After that the possibility of ascending to the pleroma-world disappears and a new age begins.

Then the time comes where such thinkers as Augustine or Scotus Eriugena appear, then the scholastics and the blossoming of European mysticism, times when the language of the mind was based on a knowledge quite different from that of earlier ages. People now sought knowledge in the physical sense-world and tried to develop concepts and ideas of the supersensible worlds from there.

But the earlier sense of the direct experience of the spiritual world, the pleroma, was gone. Human beings were meant to enter an entirely new phase of development. It's not a question of assessing the merits of ancient or mediaeval times, but of recognizing what the task of human civilization is in the various ages. So we can say that the direct experience of the pleroma evolved in ancient times, which had the task of developing that power of spiritual cognition oriented towards the spirit.

Then as time moved on, there arose out of the depths of humanity a darkness, which obscured the world of the pleroma and humanity began to cultivate faculties not known before, faculties of thinking, of reason and rationality. In those older times with the direct experience of the pleroma, people didn't develop their own thinking. They received everything through illumination, through inspiration and through instinctive supersensible perception; their thoughts were revealed to them. That thoughts would well up or spring up in your mind, that you would form thoughts with logical coherence yourself, all this emerged only later. Aristotle sensed it, but it only really developed from the second half of the fourth century CE onwards. In the Middle Ages they attempted to cultivate both thinking itself and all that's associated with it.

The Middle Ages rendered a great service to the overall evolution of humanity with mediaeval scholasticism, which developed the practice of thinking in the conceiving and forming of ideas. The scholastics developed a method of pure thinking, which has now, however, been lost again.

This scholastic method of thinking is what human beings should now be learning. However, nobody likes to do this nowadays because everything is geared towards passively taking in knowledge instead of actively struggling for it. Inner activity and the corresponding impulse are lacking in the present age. Scholasticism had this to the highest degree. This is why today someone who understands scholasticism is in a position to think much better, more deeply and more coherently than, for example, someone trained in natural science. Thinking in science is schematic and short-winded, incoherent. Really, modern human beings should learn the technique and practice of thinking from the scholastics. However, it would have to be a different kind of learning from what people like today; it would have to be an active lively kind of learning and not just memorizing ready-made subject matter or reading off the results of experiments.

Thus, in mediaeval times the task of humanity was to develop the inner soul faculty of thinking. We could even say the gods had concealed the pleroma, their own manifestation, because if it had continued to influence human beings, then Europeans would not have developed the wonderful inner activity of thinking that they did in the Middle Ages and out of which modern mathematics and other disciplines have evolved in a direct descent from scholasticism.

This is how we have to imagine it: over centuries the spiritual world had given humanity the pleroma as a gift of the heavens. Humanity perceived this world bathed in light and illuminated by ideas as a revelation. Then a veil was, so to speak, drawn over this world. In Asia they still have knowledge of the decadent remains of what was behind the veil. Europe had a sort of curtain which rose up from the earth vertically to the heavens and stretched from the Urals along the Volga, over the Black Sea and down to the Mediterranean. Picture an enormous screen erected on the edge of Europe that you can't see through. Whereas over in Asia the last decadent remains of the pleroma vision continued, in Europe there was nothing left of it and thus the inner culture of thinking developed without the prospect of the spiritual world. This gives you an idea of the development of mediaeval civilization, which brought forth such greatness out of human beings, but which couldn't see what was behind the great screen that stretched from the Urals, along the Volga, down through the Black Sea to the Mediterranean. For them the East was at most a yearning but not a reality.

Here you have not a symbol, but a real image of what the European world was and how under the influence of Giordano Bruno, Copernicus or Galilei, people wanted at least to study the earth, the ground, all that is down below. And then they founded the study of the heavens based on their study of the earth, whereas the ancient study of the earth was founded on knowledge of the heavens with the pleroma. Thus, as the light was blocked off by the world-screen, the new knowledge and the new life of humanity developed effectively in darkness.

Human evolution moves forward in such a way that when something specific is meant to develop in one area, other human prospects become dark and hidden. Behind the screen only the culture of the East developed, which was for earthly purposes decadent. In Europe Western culture was in its initial stages.

Fundamentally the European world is still stuck in this phase, but the various attempts in this darkness to reach an understanding of existence with the help of all kinds of historical knowledge, are based only on externals, masquerading as science, without any insight into the pleroma. We can find a way of looking at these things and their significance for our times when we appreciate that east of the screen the once prevalent understanding of the pleroma became more and more decadent, retreated so to speak, so that people there acquired a highly developed but instinctive spiritual culture, which increasingly took on decadent forms. In Europe the life of the soul moved down into the realm of the physical senses, which from the Middle Ages onwards became the only accessible world. Thus, beyond the screen in the Orient a culture developed that wasn't truly a culture, but which tried to magically recreate in earthly physical form what we can really only experience in the pleroma as the working of the spirit. They tried to bring the living and moving of spiritual beings in the pleroma down to earth in stone or in wood and in the way these interacted they sought to perceive such spiritual effects as would exist between beings in the pleroma. What only gods can do, they reduced to the deeds of idols in the physical sensory world. The worship of idols took the place of worship of the gods. And what we can call Northern Asian oriental magic is the degenerate version of the reality of the once revered pleroma, transferred to the physical sense world. The magic arts of the shamans and their resonance in North and Central Asia—in South Asia too, but there they managed to remain relatively free of these influences—are the decadent form of the ancient visions of the pleroma. Instead of human soul involvement with the pleroma-world of the gods, they substituted magic on the physical-sensory level. They tried to replace what the soul once achieved through inner activity with physical-sensory magic. A completely ahrimanized pleroma activity developed there and among the spiritual beings in the realms bordering the earth, which in turn affected human beings.

So if we go east from the Urals and the Volga towards Asia, then in the astral world bordering the human earthly world, in the centuries of the second Middle Ages and those of the modern era, we have an ahrimanized magic practised by certain spiritual beings who, despite being above humanity in their etheric and astral development, are below them in their soul and spiritual evolution. In the whole of Siberia, through Central Asia and the Caucasus, there are terrible etheric-astral beings practising an earthly, ahrimanized form of magic. This affects human beings too, and even though they're not skilled in these arts and can't fully emulate these practices, they fall under the influence of the world adjacent to the earth and immediately bordering the astral world.

When we describe something like this, we have to be clear that behind the myths and legends of ancient times there were always tremendous spiritual visions of nature. When in Greece they spoke of fauns and satyrs involved in events on earth, they didn't construct these beings in their phantasy, as some scholars have suggested, but from their spiritual insights into nature. They really knew them as fauns and satyrs of the astral realm adjacent to the earth. At the turn of the third to the fourth century CE all these fauns and satyrs moved over to the regions east of the Caucasus, the Urals and the Volga. That became their home and the basis for their further development.

In the West against this cosmic backdrop the faculty of thinking and a certain dialectic developed in the human soul. As long as human beings adhered to strict and pure forms of thinking, to what can only be developed internally, as in the pure thought forms of scholasticism, then they cultivated what was possible according to the principles of the guiding spirits of the earth; then they were preparing for what will develop in our present times and in the near future. But this purity of thinking wasn't practised everywhere. In the East beyond the screen so to speak, there was the urge to drag down the activity of the pleroma to the earthly level, to transform the pleroma into earthly magic and ahrimanized sorcery; to the west of the screen the pursuit of rationality, dialectics and logic, the understanding of the earthly world in ideas was mixed up with everything related to lust sensations, to the pursuit of pleasure in the world of the senses. The pure practice of reason that had developed got mixed up with earthly-human luciferic instincts.

Thus, another astral world developed immediately adjacent to the earthly one in which the striving for reason and the practice of ideals were evolving. This astral world existed in the middle of a world where people like Giordano Bruno or Galilei and others strove to cultivate earthly thinking, to discover earthly laws and techniques of thinking. In and among all this emerged the beings of an astral world, who absorbed it all and incorporated sensual feelings even into religious life, made the striving for rationality subservient to physical sensory experience. So, the pursuit of pure reason took on a physical-sensual character.

Much of what developed in the second half of the eighteenth and in the nineteenth centuries as a technique of thinking is permeated with what exists in the astral world, which pervades the world of rationality. The earthly lusts of human beings, cleverly realized and interpreted through this thinking technique, fostered in them an element that was nourishment for certain astral beings, whose aim was to use these keen and highly-evolved thought processes for understanding the earthly realm only.

Thus, theories such as Marxism arose, which instead of raising thinking up to the spiritual level, narrowed it down to the mere interaction of physical-sensory beings and impulses.

This enabled certain luciferic beings, who live in this astral sphere, to influence human thinking. Human thinking became completely infiltrated with that of certain astral beings and the Western world became just as obsessed with this type of thinking as was the East with the descendants of the shamans.

And so finally people emerged, who were obsessed with those astral beings, who brought human lust into this astute but earth-bound thinking. And on the astral plane beings emerged, who lead

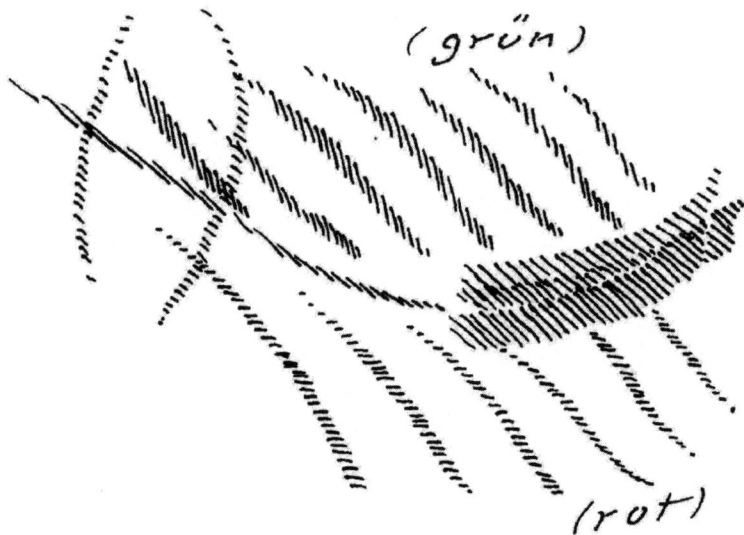

(grün = green; rot = red)

such people like Lenin and his comrades into being obsessed with them.

Thus, we have the juxtaposition of two worlds: the one to the east of the Caucasus, the Urals and the Volga, the other to the west, which form a kind of discrete astral region. We have the Urals, then the Volga and the Black Sea, where the screen once stood. Then we have to the east and west of the Urals and the Volga an astral region of the earth, in which those beings whose breath of life is this luciferic thinking of the West, and those beings east of the Urals and the Volga in the adjacent astral regions, whose life element is the earthified magic of the ancient pleroma, long for each other as if for a cosmic union. These ahrimanic and luciferic beings strive to unite with each other. And so here we have on earth a special astral territory, where also those people live whose task is to understand this. If they fulfilled the task that is entrusted to them for the whole evolutionary progress of humanity, then they would have achieved something great. But if they ignore it, then they'll become deeply influenced and obsessed with the lewd union of ahrimanized beings from Asia and luciferized beings from Europe, which was meant to take place on a cosmic level. Instead they strive towards each other with all this cosmic lasciviousness, creating a sultry astral atmosphere and causing human beings to be obsessed with them. This astral region has gradually developed to the east and west of the Urals and the Volga, directly above ground, and is the astral region of the Earth for the metamorphosed fauns and satyrs.

When we look towards Eastern Europe today, if we can perceive reality as a whole, we don't see only human beings, we see what in the course of the Middle Ages and of modern times has become a kind of paradise for fauns and satyrs who've been through a metamorphosis in their evolution. Now if we understand correctly what the Greeks saw as fauns and satyrs, then we can look at their development, at their metamorphosis. These beings have, in a way, always been in our midst, have practised their lascivious craft, consisting of ahrimanized magic from Asia and luciferized rationalism from Europe, on the astral plane and have infected human beings with it. These transformed, metamorphosed satyrs and fauns look as follows: in their lower half the form of a goat has become more feral, so that externally they have a lewd, shining goat form, but on the upper part they have an extremely intelligent head, a head that radiates light, but that is the image of all possible luciferized, rationalistic wiliness. These beings living in the faun and satyr paradise resemble something between bears and goats with an ingenious physiognomy, resembling a human being, but an extremely clever albeit salacious one. During the last centuries of the Middle Ages and the first centuries of the modern age, this region of the astral realm has become a paradise for the transformed fauns and satyrs now dwelling there.

Now while all this is going on humanity has got left behind, focussed on outworn concepts which only describe earthly reality; all the while other factors no less important than those perceptible to physical eyes and to the mind dependant on the physical body, are influencing this reality.

We can only grasp what is developing between Asia and Europe when we can understand it in its astral-spiritual aspect, when we can see how in Central and North Asia a decadent shamanism, the remnants of an earlier reality, flows over as a bawdy, degenerate magic to unite itself in a kind of cosmic bond with what has become Bolshevism. There, to the east and west of the Urals and the Volga, there is an attempt to marry sorcery and Bolshevism. What is happening there is so difficult for people to understand because it's played out in the form of myth, as luciferic Bolshevism is united with the completely decadent form of shamanism crossing over from beyond the Urals and the Volga. From the West to the East, from the East to the West, these mutually interacting events are the effects of the faun and satyr paradise. And what is influencing the human sphere from the spiritual realm is the result of the bawdy collaboration between those satyrs and fauns who migrated there in ancient times and the spirits of the West, who have only developed one-sidedly everything connected to the head.

I'll try to describe to you what is visible to a seer: spiritual cloud-like forms mass together as we approach the Urals and the Volga region, whereas the other forms remain unclear. It's as if these masses start to form clever-looking but lascivious heads; it's as if they were constantly turning into heads and losing the rest of their bodies. Then from the East, the metamorphosed fauns and satyrs appear, whose goat-nature has almost become bearlike and who lose their heads the nearer they come to the West. And then in a kind of consummation, a cosmic marriage, the beings who have lost their heads engage with those beings coming from Europe, who provide the respective heads. This is how these metamorphosed fauns and satyrs come into existence in the astral world. They're earth beings just as physical humans are. They move around in the same world as physical human beings do. They're the tempters and seducers of physical human beings because, without having to resort to argument to convince them, they can just make people obsessed with them. Also people believe that what they do originates with themselves, with their own being, whereas in truth how people behave in this field is often due to their blood being stirred up by such a being, who has brought the bear-like goat-form from the East and united it with the human head, metamorphosed into something superhuman, from Europe.

Today we have to grasp such things with the same vigour as the ancient myths were once formed. Because only when we can consciously rise up to Imagination can we understand what we have to understand if we want to take part consciously in human evolution.

Three Perspectives of Anthroposophy
I The Physical Perspective

DORNACH, 20 JULY 1923

Recently some members of the Anthroposophical Society, particularly those with a scientific background, seem to have developed the idea that there should be a back and forth of argument and counter-argument between the knowledge of the world given us by anthroposophy and what, on the basis of assumptions that emerged in the second half of the nineteenth century, is given us by science. People seem to think that it could be extremely advantageous for anthroposophy to approach and accommodate science in this way.

Especially because there is now scientific activity within the anthroposophical society, which in a certain sense is very gratifying, there have been many misunderstandings about this issue.

We shouldn't forget that in the course of the nineteenth century, under the influence of what came to be called science, general education took on a certain character, which is completely at odds with anthroposophic knowledge of the world. We have to accept that someone who's grown up with thought patterns formed by current scientific life, will have great difficulty in adapting to the anthroposophic way of thinking. So, we should be aware that we can hardly expect any endorsement of the anthroposophic world view from them.

Those people whose thought processes didn't come under the influence of contemporary science as they grew up, or who as young adults turned away again from science, are the ones who will recognize the validity of the anthroposophic world view.

To illustrate what I've just said, today I'd like to speak from one angle about the path of anthroposophy in the world. So that those friends who've had a long journey to be here today can profit from these three lectures, I want to make them as aphoristic as possible. I'll refer to various phenomena of life in modern civilization, but mainly I'd like to base the subject matter of these lectures on anthroposophic considerations.

We know what human beings experience when they go through the gates of death. Today we want to look first at the physical aspect of anthroposophy, just the first phase of life after passing through those gates. I've often mentioned how during their earthly lives a person's physical body is closely connected to their etheric body or body of formative forces, a connection maintained for their entire life on earth.

When a human being interrupts their usual earthly state of consciousness through sleep and the dream state, then they bring the astral body and the I out of the physical body and the body of formative forces. These last are so closely tied to each other that they don't separate. In a normal person the separation happens in the course of every 24 hours, so that the physical body and the etheric body on the one side and the astral body and the I on the other separate from each other, but each side forms a closely connected whole.

Now if a human being passes through the gates of death, then something different happens. First, we discard the physical body, so that for a short time there is a connection between the I, the astral body and the etheric body, which didn't exist during earthly life. This connection grants us the experiences we have, that last just a few days after death. What are these experiences?

As it melts away from us, so to speak, we see all that we have absorbed during our earthly life through our senses and also through our reason, which combines what the senses perceive.

During our earthly life when we focus our eyes towards the outside, we get used to seeing before us objects and processes taking place in colour in the outer world. And we retain these colourful impressions in our memories, even though they are fainter. We hold them in our memories. It's the same with the impressions of the other senses. And if we observe ourselves honestly, we have to admit that, in our quiet moments, when we sift internally through our memories, what we really experience inside only consists of shadowy images of external reality. In ordinary consciousness we live either in the direct, vivid experience of impressions of the outside world or in shadowy memories of them. We'll talk about what else we experience tomorrow. Today we want to be completely aware of the fact that during our earthly life our consciousness is filled with colours and colour-processes draped over objects, with sounds, sensations of warmth and cold, with all those impressions we get from our senses, and with their shadowy images in our inner soul lives, or as we could say, in our memories. We want first to look at this as a kind of starting point.

All that we experience like this melts away when we go through the gates of death. Within a few days all that filled our soul from birth to death has dissolved into the universal cosmos. We could also say: the body of formative forces or the etheric body separates from the I and the astral body, after having formed a connection with them that wasn't there before in earthly life.

Now let's look more closely at what this experience exactly is. I'll make a diagram. Let's assume that the human physical body is characterized through this diagram; the etheric body or body of formative forces is pictured here (yellow shaded area). We experience what I've just drawn, this connected form of the physical and the etheric body, only when we rest for a while in our inner selves when we wake up. We only ever experience it from the inside. And so that we can become very aware of this, I'll continue the diagram as follows and indicate the part of the etheric body that shines towards the inside with green. Since we discard the physical body after death, we don't have to pay too much attention to it here. And the part of the etheric body that shines towards the outside I'll indicate with this red colour.

Now I've said that we only experience the etheric body from the inside just after waking up, meaning we only experience the part of the etheric body that shines towards the inside here in green. We don't experience the red part that shines towards the outside.

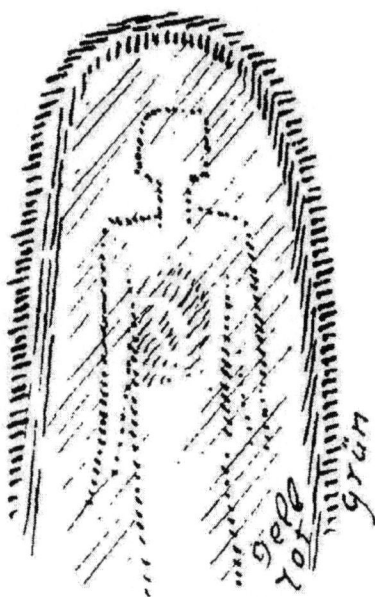

(gelb = yellow; rot = red; grün = green)

When we've passed through the gates of death the astral body and the I form a certain bond with the etheric body in the following way. You have to imagine that the whole etheric body turns in on itself like a glove does when you take the part that usually touches the skin and turn it inside out with all the fingers, so that the inside is turned towards the outside. In the diagram I have to use red for the part that in its earthly state was turned towards the outside, but now has to be drawn as the inner part. And what I draw in green is the part that was inside and now is on the outside. The whole etheric body inverts itself. However, this inversion is accompanied by a rapid expansion of the etheric body. It grows, becomes enormous and spreads out immeasurably into the universe, so that I have to depict it like this (large green circle).

Whereas with our I and our astral body we used to be inside this, now (red circle) we're across from the etheric body, which has expanded into the cosmos, but we see it from the other side. The red part, that we used to wear as a matter of course on the outside, is now turned towards the inside. The green part that was turned towards the inside and which was only meaningful in our earthly lives, is now on the outside and no

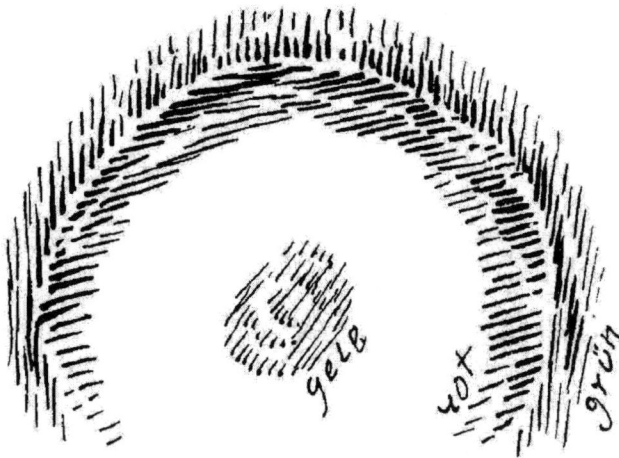

(gelb = yellow; rot = red; grün = green)

longer concerns us; it dissolves into the universe. In this green part—of course this is only a rough diagram—we find all that we've absorbed of the world during our life on earth, the sounds, colours and so on. When the etheric body inverts itself and the green part goes to the outside, we lose this green part entirely and as a result we experience a completely different world. We shouldn't think that after death we can have the same world that we had during our earthly life. This world disappears. To imagine that after death we could experience the same life, perhaps in a different version, that we had on earth is completely false. However, in comparison to earthly life what we experience through the turning inside out of the etheric body, or body of formative forces, is gigantic, but also completely different. Initially, through the fact that the outside is now turned towards the inside, we experience in powerful impressions, not comparable to sense impressions, the whole creation of our earthly lives. We don't experience the red of the rose, but how we have created an image of the red of the rose in ourselves. But there it doesn't stay quietly as it does in physical earthly life. On earth the roses in the rose garden grow peacefully side by side and you can feel at peace there with yourself. But here the rose garden becomes something entirely different; the rose garden turns into events in time. When we've let our gaze wander from one rose to another and have created the image of the first rose, then of the second, the third and so on inside ourselves, then this creation of one rose after the other as if in waves as fast as lightning, not as actual roses, but as images rolling one after the other, this appears in a sea of experience as our inner life. So now we have before us something we didn't see during life on earth: the creation, the gradual becoming of our earthly life. We know how our soul has developed from childhood onwards. But what we paid no attention to during life now passes before our inner vision. It's as if we'd stepped out of ourselves, become a second self, and now watch how we gradually formed the simple ideas of childhood, the more complex ones of old age and so on. We see how this little person develops on the inside. We see how hour by hour this earthly existence shapes itself. We even get the impression that this whole earthly life is really formed by the cosmos, because all that we see here expands out into the cosmos and, by the fact that we expand out, we realize that what was formed in us during life on earth was formed from out of the cosmos.

Now gradually we're able to see what this earthly life is all about. Let's start with what most people today believe in with regard to earthly life. Human beings eat and through this they incorporate external substances into their own organism. This is an incontrovertible fact. We also transform these substances, starting in the mouth, then moving on further down the organism. What is absorbed in this way crosses over into the whole organism, merges with it. Then science says that we also continually lose substances. You only have to consider how you cut your nails and your hair, provided you're not bald. And you can see from the flaking of the skin how human beings lose matter. Nowadays it's common knowledge that by losing tissue in this way, human beings renew themselves completely in the course of seven years.

If I were to express this dramatically, I could say that all that is sitting here on these chairs today, inasmuch as it consists of matter, was floating about somewhere in the world outside eight or nine years ago. I'll say this much: what is sitting on these chairs today can only have been gathered together in the last seven or eight years. If you were only what would have been sitting here as muscles and flesh more than seven or eight years ago—you're all no longer young so you'll have regenerated yourselves several times by now—then nobody would be sitting here.

Thus, whatever you were carrying about as muscles or blood or whatever seven or eight years ago, none of that is sitting here now. You've shed all that or cut it off bit by bit by now.

What does science with its materialistic stance say to this? It says that during these last seven years we've all eaten; what we've eaten sits here now and what we ate before that doesn't. So, for example, each person sitting here has a heart. Now the physical matter of the heart, science says, has renewed itself over the last seven or eight years, so that now, in comparison with your condition let's say nine years ago, you have a new heart. This is roughly what people think today.

But it's not correct. People only think this because they don't realize what I was talking about before and so they can't include it in their scientific observations and their scientific thinking. They know nothing about the inversion of the etheric body or body of formative forces and what it reveals to us after we've gone through the gates of death about how we developed from childhood onwards. Because when you know this, then you're in a position to see into the human organism in a very different way. And only then can you learn the truth.

You can believe that out of the cabbage, the potatoes and other vegetables, the cherries, the plums and so on, which we've eaten over the years, that out of all this the tissue of the heart has developed. But it's not true. In fact, the heart that you carry within you today doesn't essentially—and it's important that I say essentially—have much to do with the matter you've ingested over the last seven or eight years. It developed in a mysterious way out of the ether of the cosmos, which you have yourself over the last seven or eight years condensed into the heart muscle. So that the heart you have now hasn't renewed itself in the last seven or eight years out of physical matter, but out of the cosmos. You yourself have renewed your heart and your other organs out of the ether. Over the years you've actually made a new person of yourself, not from the earth upwards, but from the cosmos downwards. After death we can see all this activity of the ether body and how it functioned during the whole of our earthly life, so that we always regenerated ourselves from out of the cosmos.

Now your materialistic conscience—and all human beings have one—will say: but we did eat, we absorbed substances from outside and they went through inner processes. Yes, but these inner processes aren't as closely linked to your real deeper human being as you might believe. The matter that you've absorbed through eating, you've also discharged in one of the various ways humans do this. These substances pass through the human organism, but without essentially uniting with what humans are; they only form a kind of stimulus. We have to eat so that in an inner process something happens that stimulates us. Through this stimulation we develop an etheric activity relating to the cosmos, not to the earth. What happens with the food we eat, digest and absorb into our bloodstream is that processes develop that stimulate a corresponding etheric process as an opposing response. My old heart is stimulated by the physical but transformed matter that I ingest. But I make my new heart out of the world ether.

Now we can say something that for modern thinking sounds preposterous. You're all sitting there; what you've renewed in yourself in the last seven to eight years didn't come from the potato and cabbage fields, it existed outside in the cosmos, in the sun, the moon and the stars; it came down from there and you re-constituted yourselves from the universal ether.

This shows the mistake that necessarily follows from modern thinking. People only attempt to connect human regeneration to physical earthly matter, but not to the ether. And the result is that once you've got used to the ideas that are currently being taught in physiology, then you can't avoid regarding everything that anthroposophy teaches us as a kind of phantasy. Therefore, you have to be quite clear how fruitless it is to enter into discussions about this, how only when you're proficient in both fields, modern science and anthroposophy, can you show how they can mutually benefit from each other. But we shouldn't cherish hopes that people who are accustomed to these materialistic ideas will be readily convinced by argument—these hopes are usually to the detriment of anthroposophy. You have to be completely clear in your ideas on this score. Then you'll recognize that these people have themselves to learn the whole process of getting to know anthroposophy, before they can even begin to understand anthroposophic cognition and perception.

As I said, it's essentially the case that we regenerate our new human being from the cosmos. Obviously, we won't find those substances in the cosmos that are in our hearts, because there they are so fine that they can't be traced with physical earthly means. There they are etheric. But what appears as solid heart tissue at a certain age has been densified out of the cosmic ether. Thus, nine or ten years ago what is sitting here today was up there in the heavens, in the stars; and anything that is still there, that has pushed its way from matter into what should have been formed from the etheric, that is the reason for illness. If we're carrying physical matter in us that is too old, then this is a reason for illness. And we gain deep insight into the essence of illness when we know how matter instead of being expelled, contrives to stay put; for all matter that is absorbed as physical, earthly substance is meant to be expelled. If it remains in the organism, then it's a cause of illness.

We can only gain real knowledge by insight into those first experiences we have shortly after leaving our earthly body and this knowledge affects even the practical side of life. So, after death all our sense impressions, all the rational processes related to our sense impressions, all this melts away. We see the world very differently. Minerals, plants, animals, as we saw them before death, are all gone. How human beings develop—that remains.

We've gone through the gates of death. We've left the earthly arena. We've entered the cosmic arena and are surrounded by a different world. It's as if we've left the little cubby hole of the earth and have entered the great hall of the cosmos and we feel as if we're spread out over the cosmos, so that we truly wouldn't have room in the cubby hole we've come from. We've now entered the cosmic arena, where we'll stay until we again descend to earthly existence. And now we find ourselves in contact with a whole new world, whose inhabitants are beings of the higher hierarchies.

We have to expand these ideas that we've gained from observing human beings, to encompass all of nature. I want to describe to you how we have to do this in the following way.

Let's assume for example that we go back a long way in the evolution of the earth. There we'd encounter completely different beings and completely different earthly processes. As you know in earlier epochs giant beasts of a lower order lived on earth which no longer exist today. The whole species has died out. Palaeontologists and geologists search

1st Period   2nd Period   3rd Period

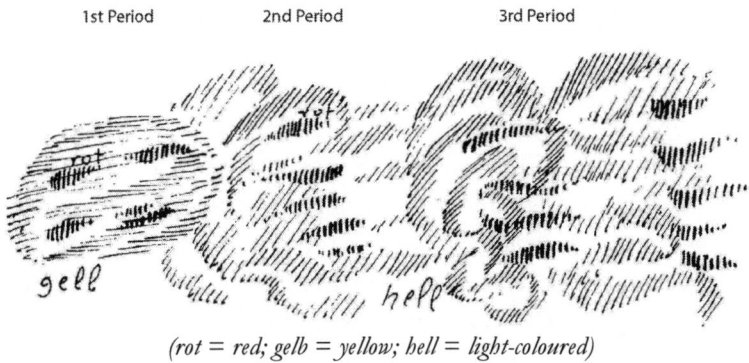

(rot = red; gelb = yellow; hell = light-coloured)

for their remains in the formations of the earth. Now I'll try to make a diagram of this ancient development, when ichthyosaurus, plesiosaurus and all these strange creatures roamed the earth.

At that time these beings weren't formed from physical earthly matter, they were formed through the cosmos, through the ether. And as the time approached when they gradually became extinct, all this ether matter, so to speak, was left over (see diagram: yellow). Now these beasts were no longer there, but all the etheric substance from which they were made remained, just as our etheric body remains. And at a later time after this etheric matter had passed through the cosmos, it was the reason for the development of other creatures on the earth. And from them in turn only the etheric remained. Out of this again other creatures were formed. And in the end the animal kingdom developed as it is today.

If we have here three consecutive periods, the first, the second and the third, then we have consecutive animal forms. But for those that follow to develop out of their predecessors, they first have to pass through the cosmos with the help of the ether, just as human beings have to pass through the cosmos between two earthly lives. And if we have beings here (see diagram: red), then they too can pass over into the ether and then, at a specific time, human beings can emerge out of the ether. But there's always the influence of the passage through the cosmos.

Now along comes a materialistic observer. They see all this and believe that the one has developed out of the other. Certainly, on earth they follow one another, but there's an etheric activity, a cosmic activity between each of them.

In the nineteenth century it became common just to look at what follows what on the earth and not to look at the cosmic activity beyond the earth. This is why the view prevails that here as a final result is the human being, before that simpler forms, before that even simpler forms and so on. This is what we can learn about the development of organisms from natural science, which doesn't allow for the etheric. Natural scientists can't see more than they can see (with physical eyes). If we accept their premise, that they don't look at the etheric, if we put the question in such a way that we're only going to look at what belongs to earthly existence, then all that is left is the physical flow of evolution. That's what the Darwinists and Haeckel did, and demanding more of an earth-bound science or even disparaging it, is nonsense. For only when we include knowledge of the etheric world can what is lacking in that theory develop. Polemicizing is pointless. If someone wants to stick to science then they can do so. And they can say to those people, who speak of other creative principles in the evolution of the world, that all that is unimportant. If they've got used to the mere earth-bound way of looking at things, then they will say the rest doesn't exist.

If we want to see things differently then we have to acquire knowledge of the etheric world. For a valid discourse with modern science there's no alternative but to say: in your own field, distinguished scientist, you are completely correct, there is no other possibility and we don't deny that. But if you want to have a discussion with us, then you first have to acquaint yourself with the basic processes of the cosmic ether; then we can talk to each other. Otherwise there's no basis for discussion.

One of the members sitting here has written a little book about botany from the perspective of spiritual science[34] and a negative review of it has been published in one of the local papers. Now how could we answer that? Imagine that you were yourself the botanist who wrote this review, having never heard of anthroposophy before and having stumbled across the second edition of this little book, then you'd write just the same things. It's perfectly natural that you'd write the same as the critic did. The fact that one of the members didn't do so and instead wrote this book on botany is precisely the reason that he started to study anthroposophy. We only need to put ourselves in the position of someone like that and we could write all these critiques ourselves. But you see if we want someone who has a certain frame of mind to be different, to be anthroposophic, then it seems to me similar to having a daughter who is blonde and suddenly wanting a dark-haired one. You can't change things just like that. What people have become through modern science can't be changed in the twinkling of an eye. We have to be realistic.

The period following the middle of the nineteenth century has shaped the human soul in a particular manner. I'd like to give you another example from a completely different angle.

You all know that there is something called analytical psychology or psychoanalysis. As I've often said here, psychoanalysis gives us some good things. But it's based on an incomplete and dilettantish view of human physiology—and on a dilettantish view of the human soul, human psychology. These two aspects interact and potentiate each other, so that psychoanalysis is dilettantism squared. If you multiply d with d you get d^2. This has a lasting effect, even if it is dilettantish, so that you can understand how all this developed out of an inadequate physiology and psychology. But this type of thinking rubs off on the souls of human beings!

Now we have an immense amount of literature on the subject. You could fill a large library with psychoanalytical literature. The authors argue vehemently in these books, so that if you follow them it can be quite interesting. Here too there has been talk of psychoanalysis[35] and we could also fill up a library with books devoted to it. But when so much has been written in this field then there must have been a lot of study invested in it. And this rubs off on the soul of human beings and dyes them a certain colour.

Now here is something very interesting: psychoanalytical literature already existed in Central Europe in 1841. This comprised only 14 lines, which said: 'In our modern, overcrowded consciousness we have to cope with many things that we can't really deal with adequately, because we just don't have the time. They remain in us as tasks, which we could do something with. As Tieck says, these are unborn souls, as if in limbo in the recesses of our souls.'[36]

So, you see these 14 lines—here they're shorter—contain the whole principle of psychoanalysis. Back then they called them unborn souls, demanding life and floating in limbo in the recesses of our souls. Now they call them provinces, soul provinces, buried deep in the soul and so on. Back then they treated this so lightly that a few lines were enough. Today our civilization has come to a point where whole libraries are full of the books written about it. But the essence, the fundamentals are all in these 14 lines. At the time, the fact that 14 lines were enough meant that the libraries were full of other subjects and people learnt quite different things than they do today.

If today a young student of psychology has to write a dissertation, then they can't avoid psychoanalysis. They have to study it. And this colours their soul. In 1841 you could express the essence in these 14 lines. No one thought it could have such enormous importance for human thinking. And so it was with many things.

It's of great significance whether or not we consider the facts when we study something. Back then in 1841 people sleepwalked through psychoanalysis. Such thoughts only occurred to this one person, Karl Rosenkranz, whose 14 lines I read to you. He once dreamt about it. Dreams dissolve and don't have such an influence on life, and people filled their waking life with other things. Today however, people sleepwalk through many things because their waking days are filled with psychoanalysis and similar themes.

We really must examine this closely, then we'll be able to say at what point we have to get involved, so that anthroposophy can be recognized in the world. At all events we can't just get into a discussion. This polemicizing is just as if someone is lying in a room fast asleep and snoring loudly, while someone else is awake and trying to convince the sleeping person of what he is saying. They can't understand. And likewise, it's not possible for two people to understand each other in the life of the mind, if both are asleep for the other's field and only awake for their own.

Obviously, there will be numerous people who are asleep for anthroposophy. And they won't be waking up to it any time soon. But it would be good if anthroposophists wake up for the others, so that they don't just have a blind faith in anthroposophy, but understand from real insight into the qualities of other fields why anthroposophy is so comprehensive and includes all that other people regard as separate. And how, because it goes beyond the narrow limits of normal areas of expertise, anthroposophy expands the horizon.

Here I've given you one of the perspectives, the one that follows when you look in more detail at the earthly world surrounding you, which melts away when you die. It's the physical perspective and if we really want to understand it, it leads us to the next level which is the etheric.

In a later lecture we'll look at the soul level and examine how human beings can wake up to the soul perspective, then we'll finish with a study of the spiritual perspective. These are the three perspectives of anthroposophy.

II THE SOUL PERSPECTIVE

DORNACH, 21 JULY 1923

REGARDING the spiritual life of our times, if we are impartial enough, we must notice that since the second half of the nineteenth century the soul has gradually disappeared. Our contemporary civilization lacks soul. And if an individual human being wishes to wake up to the inner life, then they have to do so, not by participating in the concerns of our society, but in solitude.

Generally we've abandoned the practice of observing contemporary life with any alertness. For external observation, which started in the nineteenth century, there have been any number of phenomena which should really have prompted people to sit up and take notice of what is happening in the life of the mind. But such phenomena have passed without leaving hardly a trace. If they had at least been formulated, then through being expressed in language they could have made an impression on people deep enough to wake them up. But this wasn't the case.

I'd like to start today by looking at a phenomenon, which seen superficially might only raise a smile from the one person, another might view it historically as one of many aberrant world views, the third might rage against it. But mainly I want to just try and simply formulate the facts of what I mean for you.

In the last two decades of the nineteenth century, the question of who was the cleverest person of the age became important to me. Of course such things are always relative, so I'm asking you not to take this too literally, but with a grain of salt, and to look at it as a kind of typical feature of our time.

Our age is the age of intellectualism. The intellect has developed to great heights. We have to ask ourselves what is the human intellect dependent on during earthly life? Of course the power of the intellect, the activity of the intellect depends on the human being's soul, which we'll be looking at later. And it depends on what humans have within themselves—unconsciously in earthly life—as the etheric organism, the body of formative forces, as the astral body and as the I-organization.

In the current phase of development, however, human beings haven't reached the stage of actually realizing the activity of the intellect as it lives in these three elements of human nature. If humans didn't have a physical body then the intellect would have to remain silent for the duration of earthly life. It would be similar to how a person feels when they walk towards a wall. If they go straight ahead and don't look at their hands or feet, then they see nothing of themselves. But if the wall is a mirror, then they see themselves. The intellect would be like the person who doesn't see themselves: they wouldn't be able to perceive themselves if they didn't have a physical body, which mirrors or reflects the activity. Thus in our age humans owe the magnitude of their intellect to the reflection of their inner soul activity through the physical body. People wouldn't mistake the mirror for themselves, however with the intellect they make this mistake. People mistake what is only in the physical sphere a reflection of the intellect for the intellect itself. They devote themselves to the mirror image. But then the mirror image rules over them.

In a way, people abandon themselves with their intellect completely to the physical body. If human beings managed to surrender their intellect completely to the physical body, then it would become almost perfect. But if we let our inner life hold sway, then we stumble into all kinds of feelings and desires, prejudices, sympathies and antipathies and bring them into the intellect. We make it imperfect. If however we become completely dry, sober and cold, or if, as Hamerling depicts in the *Homunculus*[37], we unite the male soullessness of the billionaire with the female soullessness of the mermaid, then we would be able to think in accordance with the physical body. Then it would just about be possible to develop the intellect to the level of perfection attainable in the current age. Then we'd learn to think in such a way that only the intellect would be active in us, as if it were an automaton and could develop itself to a high degree of perfection.

This is what I said to myself in the last two decades of the nineteenth century and I asked myself: who is the cleverest person in modern civilization, in the sense that they have perfected their intellect to this relatively high level? Now probably you're going to laugh, but I really couldn't think of anyone else as the cleverest person in our current civilization than Eduard von Hartmann[38], the philosopher of the unconscious. This is definitely not some audacious paradox of mine, but something that revealed itself to me as I studied the last decades of the nineteenth century with a certain soulfulness.

You can imagine that I'd have a great respect for the man I'd chosen as the cleverest person of the age. This is why I dedicated what I had to say about the theory of cognition in my book, *Truth and Knowledge* to Eduard von Hartmann. So I'm not speaking disrespectfully, but rather out of a deep regard. What lies behind von Hartmann's philosophy was the fact that initially he was trained as an officer. He had made first lieutenant when he had problems with his knee, so that he then started to develop the intellectuality that had been destined for militarism and transformed it, metamorphosed it into philosophy. It's interesting, that out of these beginnings there developed what I can only formulate as Eduard von Hartmann being the cleverest person of the nineteenth century.

This is why he could see so clearly what it was possible to see in the last third of the nineteenth century. He understood human consciousness insofar as it was earth-bound or tied to the physical body. Being intelligent he didn't deny the spirit. But he relegated it to the sphere of the unconscious, which not having a body, not being closely bound to but always beyond the physical, and being therefore spiritual, can only be unconscious.

You can only be conscious—so said von Hartmann—in the body. Even if the body is not everything, even if the spirit exists, it can't be conscious and thus is unconscious. Hartmann continues: when human beings go through the gates of death, they shouldn't expect that they can then achieve a different consciousness, for beyond earthly consciousness is only the unconscious. The human being then enters the sphere of the unconscious. Unconscious spirit is everywhere where there is no human consciousness.

Eduard von Hartmann's philosophy is a spiritual philosophy, but of the unconscious spirit. Consciousness only exists in the human body, even though spirit is everywhere, but it's a spirit that knows nothing of the world or of itself—an unconscious spirit.

Isn't it absolutely clear that this unconscious spirit can never penetrate anything outside itself except through the physical human body? This is clear from the start. But this tells us something very important. It tells us that this intellect, that allows itself such judgement about the unconscious, knows no love.

I'm not saying that von Hartmann knew no love, but that his intellect, which was why he distinguished himself, knew no love. A loveless intellect cannot build any bridges. Therefore it is confined to itself and can't gain consciousness. It stays in the sphere of the unconscious. We could also say: it stays in the sphere of lovelessness.

This already indicates that it's also the sphere of soullessness, for where love can't appear, soulfulness slowly disappears. And this is how we sense the loveless atmosphere of most of civilization in the second half of the nineteenth century, on whose shoulders our own culture stands.

It's remarkable where Eduard von Hartmann ended up through cultivating this unconscious spirit bound to lovelessness.

He studied this world of earthly life that gives humans their consciousness. But what would happen if we humans couldn't live in our bodies, if we couldn't come down into the body and unite with it every time we wake up? What would befall us then?

When we wake up as earthly beings, our I and our astral body, which in sleep were separated from our physical and etheric bodies, return to them. The I and the astral body reunite themselves intimately with the physical and etheric bodies and become as one with them. And as long as we earthly humans are awake, we have to speak of an intimate unity of the soul-spiritual and the physical-corporeal. However, if you separate the soul-spiritual from the physical-corporeal, as does Eduard von Hartmann intellectually, then you would have the following reality: it would be as if when we woke up and entered our physical and etheric bodies, instead of merging with them, we just inhabited them without fusing with them. According to von Hartmann, the unconscious spirit inhabits the body and becomes conscious through it during physical earthly life. If it really happened as he thinks it does, then we would enter our physical and etheric bodies when we wake up, but we wouldn't unite with them, and would only inhabit them as if we inhabited a house which we would then explore from the inside. We would be inside it but separate. What would happen then?

Now if our soul-spiritual didn't unite with the physical body and remained separate from it, then we would feel pain, which would be quite unbearable for our soul. For all pain has its origins in the fact that an organ is not functioning properly, that the organ is sick or that we've been ousted from part of our physical body. If we were totally ousted from our physical body and were just an appendage to it, then the pain we experienced would be indescribable. Every morning when we wake up, we're threatened in a way with this pain. But we manage to overcome it by immersing ourselves in the physical and etheric bodies and uniting with them.

Now von Hartmann was certainly no initiate, he was only an intellectual, albeit the best intellectual, of the second half of the nineteenth century. He just put into thought form what I've described to you as a reality. He imagined the world as being such that our I and our astral body wouldn't unite with the physical and etheric bodies. He thought the relationship of human beings to their bodies was as I've described above.

This led him to the following conclusion: he ended up in a terrible pessimism. This is the pessimism we would experience if, on waking up, we were separated from our physical body. Von Hartmann had it through thinking. What is the result of his thinking? The world is as bad as could be. The world is full of evil and pain and the only real cultural achievement that humanity could attain would be to gradually obliterate it, to destroy it. Then at the end of the *Philosophy of the Unconscious* he offers us an ideal.

Eduard von Hartmann lived in an age when technology was developing apace and when there were more and more machines to perform various tasks. If you had looked then at what was becoming possible through machines, you'd have been fascinated by their potential. And if you'd exponentiated what machines could do and what perfecting them could mean for the world, then you'd have had an enormous suggestive force.

Eduard von Hartmann surrendered himself to this suggestive force. And he thought that humanity, having now developed the intellect would become increasingly intelligent and would gradually have to realize that they must destroy this world. They would have to develop a machine, which could bore into the middle of the earth and then through some technological feat would then proceed to blow up this whole evil earth and everything on it and fling it into the furthest reaches of the cosmos.

We have to allow that the thinking of other intellectuals of that time, even if they weren't as clever as von Hartmann, was based on the same fundamentals, but that they didn't have the courage to think it through to the bitter end. And we can even say that, if we just faced what the intellect alone could give us, with no input from the rest of the world, then this ideal of von Hartmann's could seem, in a certain sense, inevitable.

I've already said that people didn't express contemporary phenomena in words. But we should try to get a real understanding of the *Philosophy of the Unconscious*, which put this proposal to humanity in 1869. Eduard von Hartmann was really much cleverer than the rest, because after putting this ideal before humanity, he actually did something which I've often spoken about. In the same book where he puts this ideal before us, he speaks of the spirit, even if it is the unconscious spirit, but still it is spirit. This was a terrible sin, because science had come as far as having banned spirit from its discourse, even in that harmless form of remaining completely unconscious.

Thus, other clever people regarded the *Philosophy of the Unconscious*, which had made quite a name for itself in the literary world, as dilettantish. So, Eduard von Hartmann played a trick on them. A rebuttal of the *Philosophy of the Unconscious* by an unknown author was published, which thoroughly disproved this spirit philosophy. The title of the book was *The Unconscious from the Perspective of Physiology and Evolutionary Theory*. This anonymous text copied the spirit—I should really say unspirit—of those other intellectuals so well, that the most distinguished scientific minds of that time, Oskar Schmidt, Ernst Haeckel and many others, wrote reviews full of praise about it and said: 'At last someone has polished off this dilettante, Eduard von Hartmann! What a pity we don't know who this anonymous person is. If they revealed themselves to us, we'd accept them as one of our own.'

Of course, after they'd all given the book lots of publicity, it promptly sold out and had to be reissued. Thus *The Unconscious from the Perspective of Physiology and Evolutionary Theory* by von Hartmann appeared in a second edition.

So, you see through this, von Hartmann proved how clever he was, because he could be clever in his own right and then he could outdo the opposition in their own field.

Yesterday I said that psychoanalysis is dilettantism squared, so as soul characteristics always potentiate themselves, today I should say that Eduard von Hartmann's intellect was cleverness squared, cleverness multiplied by itself.

We shouldn't sleepwalk past such a phenomenon of our age as we normally do. We should name it and hold it up before our souls, then we'd really see the absurdity of our times. Why was Eduard von Hartmann so clever? He was so clever because he really looked at all the notable events of his time with eagle eyes. He was in a way the natural scientist of philosophy. That's almost as if you would say: the pastry of the soup, but still you could say the natural scientist of philosophy.

Now if we want to avoid falling into these traps, then we have to look carefully where we step by examining such phenomena empirically. If we want to find our way out of the confusion of our times, then we have to look at what human beings really carry in their soul.

If we move from the physical human being gradually over to the spiritual, to the soul level, then, as we saw yesterday, we come first to the etheric body or body of formative forces.

As a child of his times, von Hartmann knew nothing of such an etheric body. He didn't go from looking at external, physical nature up to the level next to the physical, to the etheric body or body of formative forces.

We know that when a person goes to sleep, their I and their astral body separate from the physical body and the etheric body. The etheric body remains behind in the physical body. If you only use your earthly consciousness, you can never really know the nature of the etheric body. When you wake up, you immerse yourself with your I and your astral body in the etheric body. Then you're inside. Then you can only experience what you've brought with you in your I and your astral body. A being with a much more developed organization would have to come down into the etheric body while you're asleep, while the I and the astral body are outside. Such a being could really study the nature of the etheric body objectively and would be able to find the real etheric body, that you left behind with the physical body, when you fell asleep. If you could see what you left behind, you'd find that this etheric body or body of formative forces is, in a real earthly sense and also in a much higher sense, a paragon of wisdom.

If we look closely, we can see that when we leave our physical and etheric bodies at night, then the two that remain behind are much cleverer than we are when we're in them. This is because in our I and our astral bodies we're the children of earth evolution and of moon evolution. The etheric body, however, goes back to the sun stage of development and the physical body even further back, to the Saturn stage. They are at a much higher level of development. At present we can't match what our I and our astral body have developed with what the etheric body has gathered in wisdom over the course of time from the sun stage onwards. We could say that our etheric body is concentrated wisdom. Now if as human beings, we bring the wisdom of our astral body and our I into this etheric body, then we need something to reflect it back, just as we need the backing on the mirror when we want to see the reflection. We need the physical body as the backing. Just as we couldn't stand if we didn't have the physical ground beneath us, so we couldn't exist in our etheric body if it didn't border the physical body, coming up against it at every point, so that the etheric has a kind of backing in the physical body. Otherwise the etheric body, in its inner life, would be like a human being floating in space without a basis. Thus, for normal earthly life we have a soul life that lives in the etheric body but needs the physical body as a base.

At this soul level we can only access the mineral realm; we can only study the realm of the lifeless. If we want to access the plant realm, we need to be able to use the etheric body without the physical body.

How can we do this? How can we use our etheric body without our physical body? We can do this if through inner exercises we gradually develop from people who live primarily in the element of gravity through their physical bodies, to people who live through light in the element of lightness, who through light feel themselves connected not to the earth but to the vastness of the cosmos; when looking at the stars, the sun and the moon, the vastness of space becomes as familiar as looking at the plants growing in the fields. If we're just children of the earth, then we look at the plants growing in the fields and appreciate them, but we can't understand them because we're earthly human beings subject to gravity. But having developed into earth-bound beings, if we could then find a relationship to the fields of the star-studded heavens—looking not down to the ground but up to the skies—if we could feel ourselves as related to all this as we are to the earth, then by transforming earthly consciousness into cosmic consciousness, we could begin to use our etheric body just as we do our physical one. Only then would we be able to begin to understand the world of plants. Plants aren't brought up from the earth, they're drawn up from the earth by the heavens.

Goethe was filled with a longing for this as he was developing his metamorphosis of plants. And he described many aspects as if he felt himself to be a sun person instead of an earth-bound one and had sensed how the sun had drawn the growth forces in the roots of the plant out of the earth; had sensed how the sun joined forces with the influence of the air to develop the leaf; and finally how the sun then gradually refined what it had drawn out of the earth into the form of the blossom and the fruit.

You just have to read this wonderful text by Goethe, published in 1790, *An Attempt to Interpret the Metamorphosis of Plants*[39] and in several places you'll find the rudiments of this approach. Goethe yearned to understand the plant world. But he failed repeatedly to develop real etheric vision instead of physical vision. This is an impulse that Goethe already had and which, if we want to follow him and I mean not the dead man but the real live Goethe, we have to develop further ourselves.

For by sensing that when we are really conscious of our etheric body our soul can achieve something like this, we can also sense our heavenly origins, our independence from the earth and from our position on it. The human soul can say to itself: you are of cosmic origin; you're placed on earth by dint of your physical human body, but your origins are cosmic. And when you feel joy at the sight of the plant world here, then that part of you that feels this joy is a child of the heavens, who can appreciate all the flora the heavens draw up out of the earth. We humans free ourselves from the earth by really grasping our etheric body or body of formative forces.

When you do this, whereby love for the plant world is a great help, when you reach the stage of dwelling in the etheric body just as you otherwise do in the physical body, then not only do you become conscious of the etheric body, but just as through your physical body you become aware of the world of the senses, so through the etheric body you become conscious of the etheric world.

What do we sense when through our etheric body we look into the ether world, just as through our physical body we look into the physical world—what do we see there? We see what for physical reality is the past out of which this physical world has developed. We see in spirit the images of what once existed, so that the present could evolve from it.

Therefore, in ancient times the first initiation given to human beings was the initiation of the cosmos. In humanity's oldest schools they worked towards the initiation of the cosmos. The teachers of the first mysteries initiated people into this reading in the ether of the cosmos, which we could also call reading in chaos, or reading in the Akasha chronicle; reading what has passed and has created the present. So basically, the first stage of initiation that humanity attained in their earthly existence was this cosmic initiation.

We can then reach a second stage as follows. When we wake up, we let the astral body and the I sink down into the physical and etheric bodies. We ensoul the etheric and the physical bodies and unite ourselves with them. However, we can only capture as much of the endless wisdom of the etheric body as we bring to it. But it animates us continually. If we have a good idea, then it's the etheric body with its intimate connection to the cosmic ether, which has stimulated this idea. All the good ideas, the geniality that we develop in our waking life, come from the etheric body and so ultimately from the cosmos. The genius speaks with the cosmos by way of the stimulation of the astral body through the etheric body.

Even if someone doesn't understand this, it nevertheless holds true and their soul life is still made up of the connection that the astral body and the I make with the physical and etheric bodies on waking up.

When we feel equally at home with the stars as we do with the fields of the earth and make the vastness of the universe the upper foundation of our existence, then we are able to experience the etheric. Human beings always exist in it, only they can't become conscious of it without initiation. In reality everyone experiences it. When we look for a backing for our astral body, then it's always there; it's just a question of becoming aware through spiritual science of what exists in all human beings.

Let's assume you couldn't see the physical ground, but still you're standing on it. And if through scientific study someone discovered the ground and informed you of this fact, you'd still be standing on it. Whether someone who's proficient in spiritual science tells you that you're rising up to the upper ground, to the star grounds, or not, in reality you're rising up nonetheless. Thus, we humans inhabit another world through our astral body, a world of living spirit beings, the world of the higher hierarchies.

Just as when we're in the physical world, when the physical world is our reality, we're surrounded by minerals, plants and animals and this is the soil out of which we've developed, so we humans exist through our astral body in the world of the higher hierarchies. Living in this world we have the relevant backing (mirror) for our astral bodies. But we always carry this within us whether we've learnt from spiritual science or not. And we carry this within us as the capacity to feel.

All of the world that we make our own through our capacity for feeling, this most intimate soul-life, this all consists of the weaving and flowing of the spirits of the higher hierarchies in our astral body. When we become conscious of our feeling then at first we recognize an emotion, but in this feeling lives the weaving and flowing of the spirits of the higher hierarchies within us humans. We can't really grasp our soul-life if we don't sense how the soul is immersed in the spirit worlds of the higher hierarchies. The past of our world of the senses is revealed to us through etheric vision and so, if we recreate in a modern way what was developed as the initiation of the cosmos in the earliest earthly mysteries, then the soul can develop such a depth, that we can become conscious of what is going on in the astral body.

To achieve this, we have to immerse ourselves lovingly in the relationship with the spiritual worlds that lived in the great mysteries. If we learn about the cosmos under the guidance of initiation wisdom, then we'll reach the first stage of soul reality. We could enter into the processes of the mysteries and read in the Akasha records not only the past of the stars, the past of the animals, the past of physical human beings, but read also what lived in the souls of the great teachers of the mysteries. And as I've tried to describe as best I could for present-day human beings in my *Christianity as Mystical Fact*, we could activate in ourselves what the teachers of the mysteries had developed out of their interaction with actual spiritual beings, and then we'd be approaching an initiation, which in later earthly times appeared next to the cosmic initiation, and which I'd like to call the initiation of the sages.

We can speak of two levels of initiation: initiation through the cosmos and initiation through the sages. What the sages taught as cosmic knowledge is the substance of cosmic initiation. Looking into the souls of those who preceded us in the life of the soul leads to the second level of soul being. We can start with this by studying external history. If we understand, really grasp what still illuminates humanity from earlier times—for example the wonderful wisdom of the Vedanta and other ancient sources of wisdom—then in turn our own intrinsic vitality will grasp us and lead us to the initiation of the cosmos. And if we immerse ourselves intimately in what I've described in my *Christianity as Mystical Fact*, where I've tried to show the relationship of the old mysteries to the Mystery of Golgotha, then we approach the initiation of the sages.

In the present age we have to look honestly into our own inner being and without partiality really get to know our own spirit, which lights up our soul from the inside. I'll speak more about this as the third level of initiation next time. This is the initiation of self-knowledge.

When today spiritual science speaks of the soul, then it has to speak from the perspective of these three levels of initiation: initiation through the cosmos, initiation through the sages and initiation through self-knowledge. This leads us through the various spheres of soul life. But it's not possible to take even the first steps on this path without love. And I have to say that the intellect of our times, which is developed to the highest degree, completely forgets love, loses love. Because of this something specific happens.

Only by being ready to listen to the genius of our times can we respond with love to what we describe as the physical body, the etheric body, the astral body and the I. But are contemporary human beings capable of taking seriously what we mean by 'the genius of the age', as seriously as is its due? Isn't it just an empty abstract phrase for most people? Just think how far most people are from an understanding of the real living spirit, that works and lives and weaves in our time—the genius of the age, the zeitgeist.

Even though human beings deny the spirit, they are nevertheless not rid of it. The spirit is irrevocably connected to humanity. But if human beings reject the zeitgeist, then the demon of this age will appear. At the beginning of the last third of the nineteenth century, the intellect had progressed as far as following only the mechanism of the physical body and had itself become automatic and mechanical, attaining thus the highest levels and becoming extremely clever. But as the intellect developed an image of itself as mechanical and material, then it began to behave as people behave when they deny the spirit. Then the demon of the age took possession of it. The intellect had severed itself from the soul. Intellect became mechanical, soulless and created the equivalent philosophy. It didn't have love and so couldn't love wisdom (philosophy). This philosophy could only be the intellectual image of earthly demonology, an earthly demonology which imagines the ideal machine that bores down to the centre of the earth and then blows it up and out into the cosmos.

Thus spake the demon of the age, the intellect of the age. We'll often have to listen to the demon of the age, if we don't want to recognize the reality of the soul. Then the soul appears to the intellect as it would appear to human beings, if on waking up and immersing ourselves in our physical and etheric bodies, instead of uniting with them, we remained separate from them. For this intellect is a stranger to the true human being, it's made itself independent of the human being. An intellect that's connected to the human being will struggle up from earthly consciousness to higher states of consciousness. But an intellect that only connects itself to the earth, severs itself from the human being and thus has only a reflection of the intellect and will relegate all other states of consciousness to the unconscious, the endless ocean of the unconscious. The human soul ceases to be aware of its heavenly origins and of its independence from earthly life.

However, human soul life consists of this swinging back and forth from the physical to the spiritual. This pendulum is the life of the soul. If a person honestly believes that only the physical exists and, not being able to completely deny the spirit, relegates it to the unconscious, this is a denial of the life of the soul.

Hartmann mused on the nemesis of the earth, as only someone can who's asleep in the physical body but also clairvoyant in that same body and so represents the agony of the earth intellectually. Meanwhile, a friend of his, with whom he frequently corresponded, was lying ill and in real agony, as many of his physical organs wouldn't allow the soul-spiritual to unite with them. So, he experienced the agonies of the earth in reality and not just in thought and could only express the soullessness of the times as satire. This is Robert Hamerling, who wrote his *Homunculus* in the 1880s, whereby he shows the soullessness of the age in this character, who is only active in the outside world, earning more and more money and becoming in the end a billionaire. The whole terrible prospect of the soulless age revealed itself before the eyes of his soul. And Hamerling lets this soulless billionaire, the Homunculus, who was conceived and born without the participation of the soul, mechanically in a laboratory, marry a soulless elementary spirit, the mermaid Lorelei.

Robert Hamerling saw this whole prospect of the soulless age in the struggle of human beings in the world of matter, their intellect devoid of spirit, which in nature spirits is normal, but which in humans arouses all the forces of destruction right up to the demonically addictive destructive wish to blow the whole earth up and out into the cosmos. Hamerling could only deal with this problem of the soulless age as satire.

A new civilization, a new culture needs soul. We can only develop this soul when we illuminate our earthly experiences in the light of spirit knowledge.

So the cleverest man of our times has put the issue before us in the most frightening manner, and that other person, who sensed most tragically where this cleverness leads us, experienced it firsthand as physical suffering and has given us his vision as satire. Now through spiritual cognition we must transform this into the soul perspective, which we must strive to achieve.

Yesterday we talked about the physical perspective, today about the soul perspective and tomorrow we'll talk about the spiritual perspective.

III THE SPIRITUAL PERSPECTIVE

DORNACH, 22 JULY 1923

As earthly beings humans are familiar with three alternating states of consciousness. The waking state from waking up until falling asleep. Then the opposite state, which is the sleeping state, where the soul immerses itself in spiritual darkness so to speak, and has no experience of the environment. And between these two the dream state, in which experiences we've had while awake play a part, but where, through certain very significant and interesting inner forces, these waking experiences are subtly altered, as for example when something that happened far in the past seems to be in the immediate present. Or where something that passed by without our giving it a thought and which we hardly noticed in our usual waking state, then turns up in our dream life. The dream state connects things that don't normally belong together.

At the same time it's a characteristic feature of the dream state, that all that we perceive in a dream, the dream content, mostly consists of images, and even when we hear a word in a dream, then it's the image of the word that we perceive, the sound of the word, the tone modulation, all contributing to the image, an audible image, one the soul can hear.

Now there is much in a dream which can deeply preoccupy us human beings. But we can't really gain an insight into real spiritual existence if we aren't able to develop a valid concept of these three states of consciousness: waking, dreaming and sleeping.

So today with the help of spiritual science, we want to describe these three states of consciousness as far as possible. Firstly, the state of waking consciousness.

Human beings can become aware that on waking up they lead a conscious life by starting to utilize the organs of the body and of thinking, which is bound to the body. Even if they don't know that the I and the astral body descend into the physical and etheric bodies when they wake up, still they can sense perhaps in a vague, but still clearly perceptible manner, how they gradually have power over their limbs, power over their organs and the power to develop their own thinking.

All this can teach human beings how their waking life is dependent on the physical body. And when we study the etheric body or body of formative forces from the perspective of spiritual science, then we have to say that this waking life is also dependent on the etheric body, just as it is on the physical one. We have to immerse ourselves in both these parts and use this human organization in order to lead our waking daily lives.

Now if we don't begin to look at our waking lives from the point of view of spiritual science, then we can indulge in the most diverse illusions about it. We don't need to say much about the life of the senses, for what could be clearer than the fact that we employ our sense organs in our waking lives and that these sense organs communicate to us what is going on around us as a revelation of the physical world? We need only briefly examine the essence of these sense organs and we'll discover how through the relationship of the eye, the ear and the other senses to the environment, there develops as a revelation of the world of the senses what we humans call our daily experience.

What we really have to examine more closely is thinking or imagining. We should be very clear that in our thinking we have initially only an internalization of the life of the senses.

If we look at ourselves honestly, then we have to say: through the senses I receive impressions and then in my thinking I continue these impressions inwardly. And when we study our thoughts, we find that they are just shadowy reflections of what was conveyed to us by the senses. In a way our thinking is directed completely towards the outside. Thinking is the activity of the etheric body or body of formative forces, so that we can say: when we're awake and thinking as sensual earthly beings, then our etheric body or body of formative forces is directed towards the outside. But this is only one aspect of the etheric body. If we only look at what we normally have in our waking consciousness, thoughts about the outside world, then it's as if for some reason we could only look at a person physically from behind. Now imagine you would have seen a number of people only from the back. You'd have ideas about these people which you'd possibly never be able to corroborate. You'd be curious, inquisitive about what these people looked like from the front and you'd be convinced from the start that the front of them was as much a part of them as the back and that for an earthly human being the front is the more expressive part.

This is how it is when we become aware of the thinking of the world outside: we see thinking from behind. It's turned around because the direction of the flow of sense impressions in human beings is from front to back. Even where it seems to be otherwise, we have to think of it in this way: what is physically represented as being the front, that is for our thinking the back. And basically, we have to put ourselves in the position of looking at human thinking from the other side, where it's not turned towards the impressions of the senses, but shows us its hidden inner aspect.

Then, however, we arrive at something very strange. Then thinking no longer presents itself as it does when we fill our consciousness with sense images of the outside world. Seen from this aspect, our thinking, which is made up of the power of the etheric body or body of formative forces, transforms itself into forces which build up our physical organism, the creative forces in our physical organism.

When we grow, when our organs are built up from their germinal state and are formed three dimensionally, this is the other side of thinking, which emanating from the etheric body actively intervenes and works on our organization. What works and lives in us when we grow and when we metabolize our food, what appears in us as formative forces, this is the other side of thinking. Ordinary thinking only produces shadowy thoughts in us; it's the rear aspect of thinking. However, what gives our thinking apparatus its form, what shapes our brain and our entire nervous system is the creative power of thinking, and at the same time this is the creative power of the etheric body or body of formative forces. This is the other side.

It doesn't need much clairvoyant power to become aware of how, in human beings, this power of thinking works as a force of growth, as a formative force. You only need to give yourself a bit of a shake and then you realize that thinking is not just a shadowy image of the outside world, but an inner activity. You just need to turn away from this orientation to the outside, turn towards the inner activity, towards your thinking, then you become conscious of the activity of thinking.

In grasping the act of thinking we can begin to understand what human freedom is: understanding freedom is the same as realizing the activity of thinking. Hence by understanding the activity of thinking, we also realize true morality which flows through and permeates human beings.

Realizing thinking as an active element and understanding pure thought as something other than just letting our thinking fill up with sense impressions, this turning away from the external to the internal, was what I tried to make clear in my *Philosophy of Freedom*. I wanted to show how we humans can grasp this thought activity inwardly and how, in making the inner leap to pure thinking unencumbered by sense impressions, we also grasp morality as something which can blossom in pure thinking. In this way we achieve freedom consciousness.

Thus our human thinking in its initial form just shows us shadowy images of the outside world of the senses; but if we let it turn around in front of us then it becomes the creative forming force of human beings themselves, the inner activity and bearer of freedom and, as such, of what we can glimpse as moral impulses in the human entity.

In this way we progress spiritually from the physical body to the etheric body or body of formative forces. So, the first step into the spiritual world is to really experience the feeling of freedom.

Now let's look at dream consciousness. Dreams can be chaotic, they can be frightening and scary, they can be sweet, but they're always living and weaving in pictures that they conjure up before the soul. If we ignore the content and just look at the drama of the dream, then we see how, on waking up or on falling asleep, the soul lives and weaves in these dream images.

Here a certain soul force expresses itself. We could argue about whether these images are true or false, but the fact that they could be formed at all shows us that there is a force in the soul which generates them. There is an inner force which puts these dream images before the soul. There is an inner weaving soul-power which generates dreams.

Look for a moment at the process of waking up. As you emerge from the darkness of sleep, you can feel the existence of this inner weaving power. But then it submerges itself in the physical and etheric bodies. If this didn't happen then you'd continue dreaming. It's the power of the astral body. The astral body, which outside the physical and etheric bodies is not able to become conscious of itself, begins to sense itself, to sense its own power, on waking up, when it feels the resistance of the physical and etheric bodies as it submerges itself. In dreams it appears to be chaotic, but it's the soul's own power, which lives in them from falling asleep until waking up and then submersing itself. This means the power behind dreams flows out into the physical and etheric bodies. It submerges itself in the blood circulation and in the tonus of the muscles and in the etheric body too. These processes amplify the power of dream creation, which left to its own devices is only weak and impotent. The dream images just scurry about when the power of dream creation is on its own, but when it unites with the physical and etheric bodies and can use their organs, then it becomes a strong force.

What does this force do when it becomes stronger? Well, in humans it develops memory. Memory is none other than the creative dream force which has submerged itself in the physical and etheric bodies. The dream descends into the physical body and is integrated into the physical world order, so that it's no longer chaotic but forms memories, the content of memory in the physical world.

We wouldn't be able to remember anything if we didn't bring the power of dreams back from sleep into the physical body; for in the physical body the creative dream force becomes the power of memory.

When you sit there quietly, not focussed on the external world of the senses, and let your memories pass by, those memories which just emerge and perhaps comfort you or make you happy, other memories which inspire fantasies—when you do something like this, then it's the creative dream force strengthened by the physical and etheric bodies, which is active in you. This is the same dream force which when the astral body was outside the physical and etheric bodies, was immersed in the spirit of the world and experienced there the mysteries of all things.

If when you were asleep you were able to experience this same power, which in the waking state forms your memory, completely unfurled outside of the physical and etheric bodies, then you wouldn't have the chaotic images of dreams, which only develop in those moments when the astral body descends into the physical and etheric bodies. You would be immersed in the outside world, asleep and free of the physical and etheric bodies, experiencing yourself in a majestic world of images.

This world of images would be the cosmic reflection of what appears when you sit quietly and let memories appear and disappear. Your life of memories is the microcosmic mirror image of that gigantic, majestic, macrocosmic weaving and flowing of images, which our dream force goes through when the astral body is immersed not in the physical and etheric bodies, but in the phenomena and processes of the external cosmos.

When we speak of the spiritual content of our souls, we find that it mainly ebbs and flows with what lives in the memories that we've formed from the sense impressions of the world outside, and which touched our innermost selves: basically all the good times and the tragedies, all that made us happy or that made us suffer. So when we look at the soul-spiritual content of our memories, we should wake up to the reality that we owe all this to the fact that the force of dream creation, which is actually related to the cosmos, can descend into our inner being, and what lives and works in the cosmos as formative forces becomes internalized in human beings as the soul-powers of memory.

We can feel connected in our powers of memory with all the creative and active forces of the cosmos. And we can say: if I look out at how in spring the plants start to grow and how in the forests the trees develop out of seeds over years and tens of years, and when I look up at the clouds and how they change under the influence of the more external forces of form, or how the mountains form and erode, when I look at the work of all these formative forces right up to the stars, then I can say: in my soul I have something related very closely to all that. In my soul I have the powers of memory and these are the microcosmic images of what works in the outer world and weaves in the metamorphosis of all things.

Now let us look at the I, which in the sleep state also leaves the physical and etheric bodies and connects to cosmic phenomena and processes. We then become aware of how we humans are able to immerse ourselves in things with our underlying being, even if we only experience it unconsciously when we're outside. Then the I itself emerges from deep sleep and comes down into the physical and etheric bodies. And here only someone initiated into spiritual science can follow it. The descent of the dream force into the physical body as memory gives our ordinary consciousness an indication of what is happening. However, only when we have developed imagination, as I've described in my book, *How to Know Higher Worlds*, can we now learn to observe how the I, which between falling asleep and waking up dwells in the phenomena and processes of the cosmos, then descends into the physical and etheric bodies. In the present phase of human earthly evolution this I is so powerless that when they fall asleep people are immediately submerged in utter darkness, the darkness of the soul; but when this I descends into the physical and etheric bodies, it is strengthened through them and can seize and utilize the blood vessels and the innermost power of the blood and work through them.

This too has its expression in our waking consciousness during the day. The I, which has immersed itself in the physical and etheric bodies, can then express itself. The I is what lives and weaves in human beings as freedom and it is free to express itself or not to express itself. But when it does, then its characteristic expression is the human power of love.

We would never be able to blossom in love for another being or a process, in a sense to become one with them, if our I didn't actually

leave us every night and immerse itself in the phenomena and processes of the outside cosmos. It really does immerse itself in them.
By slipping back into us as we wake up, it gives us the inner power
to love, which it has attained outside. This is what appears in the
deepest innermost parts of the soul as a threefold power: freedom,
memory, the power of love.

Freedom is the primordial inner form of the etheric body or body
of formative forces. The power of memory is the creative dream
force of the astral body when it is active within us. Love is the power
which appears within us and leads us to devote ourselves to something outside ourselves.

By sharing in this threefold power the human soul steeps itself in
the life of the spirit. By developing these three powers, the sense of
freedom, the power of memory, through which we connect past and
present, the power of love, through which we can devote our inner
life to something outside ourselves and become one with the outside
world, our soul becomes spiritualized.

If we understand this with the appropriate inner attitude, then
we realize what it means that we human beings bear the spirit in our
souls. And if we don't understand this threefold inner spiritualization of the soul, then we can't understand how the human soul holds
the spirit.

This extends also to life in general. If we're capable of estab-
lishing an inner connection between memory and love—our life of
memories through the astral body, love through the I—in certain
cases wonderful things can happen.

This is how we can realize these things directly in our lives. We
remember someone we loved long after their death. We carry their
image in our souls, that means we add to those sense impressions
we had of them while they were alive what remains to us since these
last were denied us. In memory we continue our life with the dead
person with all the intensity and strength of our soul without having
any support through the external impressions of the senses. Now
we try to make these memories so vibrant that it seems to us as
if the dead person is actually there and full of life. We still remain
aware that this is all through memory, but afterwards we connect this

power that has developed through the strengthening of the astral body with the power that we have through our I, the power of love. We sustain the intense love we had for the dead person beyond the grave. We make ourselves capable of connecting the power of love with the image, which doesn't receive any more sensual stimulation, in the same manner as if we developed this love further with the help of sense impressions.

In this way we can strengthen what the astral body and the I are otherwise only able to express when they use the organs of the physical body. When we keep the memory of the dead person alive, a memory which can no longer be stimulated by the physical body and etheric body, if we keep it so active and alive that we can relate to it with intense love, then this is a way of cutting the astral body and the I loose to a certain extent while remaining awake. Especially in the memories of the dead that we're able to preserve, there lies the first stage of the liberation of the I and the astral body from the physical and the etheric bodies, while still remaining awake.

If people understood what keeping memories alive means, what it means to contemplate the image that remains of the dead person, to regard it just as we regarded it when the person was alive, then they would experience in this a path leading to the threshold that lies between the physical and the spiritual worlds and to the astral body and the I becoming free. This is the kind of jolt which the following experience shows. First, we have the living memory, as if the dead person were still there. We know that through our waking consciousness we can connect to this image with the love, that we'd normally only have if we had the sense impressions we received from them when they were alive. The jolt happens when we are able to develop the necessary inner strength. There is a jolt and we cross over the threshold to the spiritual world. The dead person can now be with us in all reality.

This is one of the ways into the spiritual world. It is connected to what we can only regard with reverence, what we can only experience in reverence and with a certain grave inner bearing.

If we let the seriousness associated with ideas, such as I've just described in the case of crossing the threshold to the spiritual world, work on our souls, if we truly realize this gravity, then we can get an idea of the seriousness inherent in entering into the spiritual world. We will have to have experienced through our own free will the profound seriousness of life, if we truly want to enter the spiritual world, truly want to understand the spiritual world.

This is what the science of initiation has wanted to impress upon external civilization throughout the ages. This too is what our so externalized times really need.

It's a curious phenomenon that today dogmatic science is more important to people than reality. In each moral deed humans can become aware of their freedom. And just as we experience red or white, so do we as human beings experience freedom. But we deny it. We repudiate it under the influence of modern science. Why? This is because modern science only wants to look at the mechanical, where the earlier event is always the cause of the later. And science dictates that everything has its cause. Causality dictates this as dogma and as causality must be right because people swear by it, so they have to deaden their sense of freedom. Reality is plunged into darkness to perpetuate the dogma, in this case the dogma of external science, which exercises such authority over people.

Science does away with life. If life became conscious of itself in human beings then this life would grasp freedom directly in the activity of thinking. Thus this purely external science, built on causality alone, is the great slayer of the life sense of human beings. We have to be aware of this.

Can we then hope that when people abolish their experience of freedom, they can still gain access to spiritual form, to the spiritual gestalt of memory? Can we then hope that such a person can recognize in memory the creative cosmic weaving power of dreams, just as they recognize the working of the colour red in the red rose? Can we hope that such a person can achieve knowledge of the second stage, when already at the first stage they've killed off their sense of freedom because of the dogma of causality? Such a person fails to discover the spirituality of their own soul. And they can't reach down to the depths where it becomes clear that, apart from its capacity to live outside among cosmic phenomena during sleep, in the spiritual world the I can learn to love through the spirit. The ultimate basis of love lies in the spirit-forged I, that descends into the human physical and etheric organism. Realizing the spiritual nature of love means also in a certain sense realizing the spiritual itself. Who realizes love, realizes spirit. But in realizing love you have to go as far as realizing the inherent spiritual experience of love. This is precisely where our civilization has completely lost its way.

Memory is a living weaving in our innermost soul and here the differences aren't as clear and profound. Only mystical spirits such as Swedenborg, Meister Eckhart, Johannes Tauler can sense the living weaving eternal spirit, when they steep themselves in memory and speak of the spark of inspiration that lights up in human beings when they become conscious of memories. Inside these memories live microcosmically the same creative formative forces which live and weave outside and lie dreamlike behind all cosmic existence. Things aren't as clear there.

But they become clear when we go up to the third stage, where we see how in this third stage our civilization has failed to recognize the primeval spiritual reality and activity of love. All spiritual phenomena have, of course, their external sensual form as the spirit immerses itself in the physical. It embodies itself in the physis. But if it then loses awareness of itself and only perceives the physical, then it believes that what is really inspired by the spirit is inspired by the physical. This is the delusion of our age, which doesn't know love. There are only fantasies about love, lies even. When thinking of love, our age knows only eroticism. I'm not saying that the lonely don't experience love—for in their unconscious feeling, in their unconscious will, human beings deny spirit much less than in their thinking—but when people in our modern civilization think or speak of love, then they're really speaking of eroticism. And we could even say that if we peruse contemporary literature, wherever we find the word love, really we should substitute the word eroticism. This is all that thinking doused in materialism can know of love. It's the denial of spirit which makes the power of love into an erotic force. In many fields not only has the genie of love had to give way to its lowly servant eroticism, but in many places now its opposite, the demon of love has appeared. The demon of love is spawned when what is divinely ordained in human beings is taken over by human thinking; this intellectuality tears it away from the spirit.

So, the descent sequence is as follows: we recognize the genius of love, we have spiritualized love. We recognize the inferior version, eroticism. But we gravitate to the demon of love. The genius of love has its demon, not in the original gestalt, but in the interpretation of sexuality through modern civilization. How often today, when they try to approach love, do people speak not even of eroticism but only of sexuality!

The discourse on sexuality in contemporary society consists mainly of what people like to call sex education. In this modern intellectu- alized discourse on sexuality dwells the demonology of love. Just as the genius that the age should be following appears on another level as its demon, because the demon manifests itself where the genius is denied, so it is in this sphere, where spirit is meant to appear in its most intimate form, in the form of love. Our age often worships not the genius of love but the demon of love and mistakes the spirit of love for its demon in sexuality.

This sphere is predestined to be completely misunderstood, for what originally lives in sexuality is permeated with spiritual love. Humanity, however, can fall short of this spiritualization of love, especially in this age of intellectualism. For if the intellect takes on the form I spoke of yesterday, then the spirituality of love is forgot- ten and only its external form is given credence.

Human beings are capable of denying their own true being. They deny it when they sink down from the genius of love to the demon of sexuality. Now I do understand the way people feel about these things in our present times.

When we think about this then we have to say to ourselves: anthro- posophy can be a guide not only for our thinking, but also for our innermost soul being and soul life and to rediscovering spirit deep in our soul. We can become intimate with anthroposophy and we do this when we know how to embrace it in its full reality.

Today someone suggested that we should develop an image or something similar of anthroposophy. But does such an image exist in reality? Do we need an image? What we really need is to become intimate with anthroposophy in innermost sincerity. Then it can permeate the whole inner fabric of our soul life, our soul being. We shouldn't try to make an external image for ourselves. Rather we should become intimate with this living being, anthroposophy, which if we are united with each other as people who understand these things, should be walking among us.

If we really live with anthroposophy as an actual being, which in a higher sense walks among us, if we ourselves are authentic and intimate with anthroposophy, then the impulse will arise in us to really experience what humanity needs to experience so very much in our present age: not just an image for the eyes of the soul , but heartfelt love of the being of anthroposophy. This is what we need and it could be the greatest impulse for our times.

I've tried here to add to the physical perspective and the soul perspective, that I described previously, the spiritual perspective of anthroposophy. The spiritual perspective isn't an external tracking of the spirit, but just the opposite, experiencing anthroposophy in the most intimate depths of the human soul and the human heart. And this deep, intimate experience of anthroposophy in the human soul and in the human heart is precisely the meditation that leads us to a real encounter with anthroposophy.

I've attempted to present the three perspectives of anthroposophy to you: the physical perspective, the soul perspective and the spiritual perspective.

The Dream World As A Transition Between The Physical-Natural World And The World Of Ethical Considerations

DORNACH, 22 SEPTEMBER 1923

IF we want to integrate what we've learnt about the stages of the path to the spiritual world into our knowledge of ordinary life, then we have to be able to properly evaluate the three states of consciousness that humans experience in their normal lives. We've already described these three states of consciousness as the waking, the sleeping and the dream state. We also know how the state of wakefulness is really only possible for human beings in their thinking, in their ideas; and that feelings, which when we experience them seem different from the dream state, are nevertheless the same basic condition. We experience feelings in the same indeterminate way that we experience dreams and even the way they're linked together is similar to dreams.

In dreams one image leads to the next. The dream isn't concerned with how things are connected in the world outside; they have their own coherence. Basically, feelings are just the same. And if in normal consciousness someone's feelings were the same as their thinking, they'd be a terribly unemotional person, a dreadfully dry and glacial human being. In the world of ideas, when we're fully awake, we have to pay attention to what we normally see as logic. We wouldn't get very far in real life if we always felt everything the way we think of it.

Then as we've often mentioned, there's the will, which emerges out of the hidden depths of our existence. We can imagine it, but its real essence, how it lives and moves in the human organism remains unknown or unconscious for us, just as do the experiences we have in sleep. If human beings experienced what the will actually does, they'd be extremely disconcerted.

The will is actually a process of combustion, of consumption. If we always had to experience how we consume our own organism in the process of willing and how we have to replenish what it has consumed with food or with sleep, this would not be a pleasant process for our ordinary consciousness.

In a certain sense we can juxtapose the images that arise when we're awake in the human realm of feeling with waking dreams and with the dream world when we're asleep or half asleep. At first, we experience these images as if they don't belong to our I but to the world outside. People who are dreaming experience the dream images so strongly as being of the outside world that they can sometimes see themselves in their dreams.

But what especially interests us in these dream images today is that when we're just going about our normal lives, one experience follows the other. In a dream, however, all these experiences are mixed up together. The dream pays scant attention to what human beings experience in their waking state as the chronology of events. The dream is a poet with all kinds of fancies.

One philosopher[40] said that he himself often dreamed that he'd written a book, that in reality he hadn't, but in the dream, he believed he'd written it and that it was better than all the books he'd written so far. However, he dreams that the manuscript is lost; he can't find it; he's mislaid it. Now he's running from one desk drawer to the next; he searches everywhere, but he doesn't find the manuscript. In the dream he has the uneasy feeling that he's lost the manuscript of his best book and maybe he'll never find it again. With this uneasy feeling he wakes up. Of course, this is a crushing dream for the philosopher I'm thinking of, who had written many books. He'd published so many that once when I was a visitor in his house as his wife was also present, she said to me: 'Yes, my husband writes so many books that the one always competes against the other.'

In this philosopher's house there was always a remarkable sense of the practical, so that once when I was visiting[41] with a publisher, I was irritated because I wanted to discuss epistemological problems with him. Now I'd brought this publisher with me, although really he'd just latched on to me, and the philosopher started in right away: 'As you're in the business, can you tell me how many copies of this book or that'—I've forgotten which—'are available in the antiquarian bookshops?' So, he was a practical person. I'm not looking down on him; I just want to show you something typical of him. Somebody else would dream something different, which would have its own particular fantasy world.

As we all know dreams don't follow our outside reality, but create their own interconnections. On the other hand, we all know too that our dreams are intimately connected to what we really are as human beings. In fact, many dreams are really reflections of the insides of our bodies and we weave into dreams what really is intimately connected to us.

Gradually we can become aware of how the dream organizes events in its own way. If we look at it in all clarity then we can slowly realize that it is we ourselves who live in these dreams. But we live in these dreams just at those points where we're either leaving the physical and etheric bodies, or when we're coming back into them. Dreams actually take place in these transition periods between waking and sleeping, sleeping and waking. I've often given examples which show that the most important part of dreams happens mainly during waking up or falling asleep. I've shown some typical examples of this—you'll remember. A student dreams that two students are standing at the door of the lecture hall. One says something to the other which according to their code of behaviour demands satisfaction. So there has to be a duel. He dreams it all colourfully: going out to the duel, choosing seconds, and so on, right up to the actual shooting. He hears the bang just as he wakes up, but it transforms itself into the bang of a chair which he has knocked over onto the floor. Just at this moment he wakes up. The chair falling over has triggered the whole dream. The dream has taken place at the moment of waking up, it only seems as if it's taken time because it has its own time in itself. Some dreams last so long according to their own inner timescale, that we can't even have slept as long as the dream seemed to last. Still dreams are intimately connected to what we experience internally as human beings, inner experiences right down even to the physical body.

People of other ages knew this very well and for a certain kind of dream—you can read this in the Bible—the ancient Jews said: 'God has punished you in the kidneys.' So, they knew that a certain kind of dream was related to the kidney function. On the other hand, you only need to read something like *The Seeress of Prevorst* [42] and you'll see how from a dream someone actually describes their own organ deficiency, someone with a particular disposition, so that a sick organ is symbolized in mighty images. This can also lead to the remedy appearing in the dream as well as the sick organ. In ancient times they even made use of this, so that the sick person was induced to reveal the cure in their own dream interpretation. We should also study the practice of temple sleep in relation to this.

When we look at the whole relationship of the dream to external events, then we have to say: the dream is a protest against the laws of nature. From waking up until going to sleep we live according to natural laws. The dream doesn't bother with the laws of nature. In a sense the dream thumbs its nose at natural laws. What makes up natural law for the external physical world isn't the law of dreams. Dreams contain in themselves a lively protest against natural law. If on the one side we ask nature what is true, it will answer in natural laws. If on the other side we ask the dream what is true, it won't answer in natural laws. If someone judges a dream by the laws of nature, they would have to say that the dream lies which it does in this ordinary sense. But the dream gets close to the supersensible, the spiritual in human beings, even though the dream-images belong to the unconscious as we would call it abstractly. And we can't judge the dream properly if we don't know that it comes close to the inner spiritual reality of human beings.

However, this is already something that our age can barely acknowledge. People want the dream to be abstract. They only want to evaluate it on the basis of its inherent fantasy. They don't want to see that in a dream we have something that's related to the innermost part of the human being. For if the dream is related to the innermost part of the human being and also protests against the laws of nature, then this is a sign that the inner human being itself protests against the laws of nature.

I would ask you to take this very seriously: when we get to know human beings, we see that their innermost part protests against natural laws. What does this mean?

When today natural scientists observe the laws of nature, which are outside, as if they were inside the laboratory, their scientific thinking does the same with human beings and treats them as if these natural laws were inside them, or better, would extend to the inside of the human being, underneath their skin, so to speak. But this isn't the case at all. The dream with its repudiation of natural laws is much closer to the inner human being than are these laws themselves. The innermost part of the human being doesn't act or function according to natural law. The dream, which in its composition is a reflection of the inner human being, bears witness to this. And for someone who understands this, it's simply absurd to believe that in the heart or in the liver the same laws apply as in outside nature. To outside nature, logic applies. But the dream belongs to the inner human being and whoever calls a dream fantastic would by the same token have to call the inner human being fantastic. They could rightfully say that, for if we look at how the inner human goes on in earthly life between birth and death, where from one side sickness appears, from the other good health, then this is much more similar to a dream than to any external logic. But our modern thinking lacks this way of approaching the innermost human being, because it's completely wrapped up in what it can observe in outside nature or in the laboratory. People want to find the same phenomena in human beings too.

It's extremely important that we learn to recognize how science treats the physical processes in the human body. We know, for example, that basically there are human proteins, fats, carbohydrates and salts. How do scientists treat this? They analyze the proteins and find a certain percentage of oxygen, of nitrogen, of carbon. They analyze the fats and carbohydrates and so on. We now know how much of these substances are in each component. But you will never learn from such an analysis how for example the potato has influenced European culture. There is no reference to this influence of potatoes in the European diet on the culture, because in this analysis you'll only find how carbon, nitrogen and so on are divided between the various foodstuffs. However, you'll never find how rye, for example, is digested by the forces of the abdomen, but that potatoes use the upper forces including those of the brain, so that when someone eats a lot of potatoes, they have to use their brainpower to digest them and consequently lose brainpower for thinking.

It's precisely in such things that we can see how neither modern materialistically-minded science nor contemporary theological thinking even come near the truth. Science describes the foodstuffs as I would describe a watch: silver is extracted from the silver mine in such and such a way. Then the silver is loaded onto vehicles and brought into town and so on. But when we reach the watchmaker that's the end of it: we don't go looking into his workshop. Then we describe the dial of the watch, which is made of porcelain and again we finish up at the entrance to the watchmaker's workshop. This is what modern scientists do with foodstuffs: they analyze them. And their results give us no information about the significance of those foodstuffs for the human organism. Despite all this analysis, it makes a great difference whether we eat the fruit of a plant as with rye or wheat, or whether we eat the tuber as with potatoes.

The human organism digests tubers quite differently from fruits or seeds. So, we can actually say that this way of thinking doesn't understand material existence. Thus, materialism is a world view which doesn't even know matter and its effects. We need the light of spiritual science in order to really understand matter. This is why the materialistically minded say that anthroposophy is spiritual phantasy. Then there are those who have theosophy or theology and want to stick with a kind of reduced spirit, which never really creates anything, which never gets as far as actually revealing how it influences material processes. They say anthroposophy is materialistic, because its insights reach right down into the material world.

This is how we're attacked on two fronts, both from those who like to treat everything abstractly and from those who like to treat it all as matter. But those who treat everything abstractly don't get to know the spirit and those who treat everything as matter, don't get to know matter. This way of thinking, which is developing more and more in our times, doesn't do justice to humanity.

Now something quite strange has been happening in our spiritual development recently. People can't help but accept the dark side of spiritual life, if they don't want to appear completely contrary. There is something typical about the manner in which people who are totally absorbed in the natural sciences behave when they're confronted with these dark areas of spiritual life, or at least—I'll get to that in a minute—when they can't completely deny it.

A memorable example of this is Ludwig Staudenmaier's book, *Magic as an Experimental Science*[43]. It's almost as if you would say: The nightingale as a machine! But still this book was written in and is typical of our times.

How does he go about it? The curious thing about him is that his life drove him to experiment with magic practices on himself. One day, out of some dark twist of fate, he just had to start experimenting on himself. He couldn't deny, for example, that automatic writing existed as he'd seen it for himself. As you know I don't recommend such things and always point out their dangerous aspects, but when a medium does automatic writing something quite remarkable happens and we have to be careful to distinguish truth from fallacy. Now this writing down of things that the person doesn't have in their head at the moment of writing, this automatic writing, became for Staudenmaier an experimental problem and he started to try it out himself. And behold, he wrote things that he never would have thought of himself. He wrote the most curious things. Just think, it's quite a surprise for someone whose thinking is completely along the lines of natural science, when they try this automatic writing, thinking nothing will happen. Then suddenly the pen has a power of its own, starts to guide the hand and writes all kinds of things that are a complete surprise. This happened to Staudenmaier.

What surprised him most is that the pen was temperamental—that's how people describe it—just as dreams can be temperamental—and it wrote things completely different from what he was thinking. From the context we can see that the pen was exerting control and guiding the hand, so that it wrote things like: you're a birdbrain!

Now that's something he definitely wouldn't have been thinking himself! And after such things kept happening and the pen had written the most amazing things, Staudenmaier asked it: 'Who is really writing here?' And the pen replied: 'Spirits are writing here.' In his opinion this couldn't be true of course, because spirits don't exist for a scientific thinker. What should he think now? He can't say the spirits have lied to him, so he says it's his subconscious, which is lying all the time. This is disastrous, don't you think, when your subconscious is convinced that you're a birdbrain and even writes it down, so you have it, as they say in everyday life, in black and white?

Nevertheless, he continued to act as if spirits were speaking and he asked them why they weren't telling the truth. And they answered: that's just our way, we're the sort of spirits who have to lie to you; that's just our character, we have to lie.

This was utterly typical. Now, however, the whole thing begins to get quite awkward, because when it turns out that truth sits up here and down below, they're lying for all they're worth, then that's an extremely uncomfortable situation. And if you're trapped in the world view of natural science, then you can't really come to any other conclusion than that this terrible liar is a part of yourself.

Still Staudenmaier sticks by his view that it can't be objective spiritual beings speaking, but only ever his subconscious. You can always stuff everything into such general concepts.

But it's also characteristic that these spirits didn't guide Staudenmaier's hand to write down a new mathematical proof or the solution to some other scientific problem. It's quite typical, that they always write about other things.

Staudenmaier already had every reason to be quite beside himself and then a friend who was a physician, advised him to go hunting. Medical advice often takes such a form. A popular prescription is that someone should get married. In this case it was that he should go hunting, so that he'd be distracted from these crazy ideas.

However, even though he did as he was told and went hunting magpies and described in detail how he was always on the lookout for the birds, he saw instead all sorts of demonic figures looking down from the trees. For example, on one branch sat a strange figure which was half cat and half elephant, thumbing its nose and sticking its tongue out at him. If he looked away from the trees and at the grass, then he saw not hares, but all kinds of fantastic figures, making fun of him.

So now it wasn't only the pen that had written something down, but his power of phantasy was now so animated that instead of magpies, demons and other kinds of spectres had started to appear. But again, these must be lies. Basically, what he was seeing was just like in a dream and if his will had stayed intact, then he might have shot not a magpie but one of those apparitions, half cat, half elephant. When it then fell off the branch it would have again transformed itself and become half frog, half nightingale with a devil's tail.

In any case we can say that a world very similar to a dream world has opened itself up to this experimenter and this world is also a protest against the laws of nature. What would have been the scientific process? He would have lowered his rifle after shooting a magpie and there would have been a magpie on the ground. However, this didn't happen; rather the night or dark side of the spiritual world, into which this man had stumbled, protested against natural laws. And if he'd stuck to his subconscious theory, this man should at least have said: if all this is subconscious, then my subconscious is protesting against the laws of nature. What is his subconscious actually saying to him? It's conjuring up all kinds of demons as I've described. So, it's saying something very different from what he himself has developed in his thinking. At the least he should come to the conclusion that if the world was organized only according to natural principles, then his inner self couldn't even exist and he couldn't exist as a human being; because when this inner self speaks, it speaks very differently from what is contained in natural laws. So inside us human beings there is a completely different world than that which is governed by natural laws, a world that even protests against these laws.

Anyway, this is the most interesting thing about this experimenter or this experimenting magician, who managed to impress quite a number of people. It shows us how it's actually possible with other methods to arrive at a perception of a world that is part of our lives, such as the dream world and all that belongs to it.

And examining our ordinary lives in the right way shows us that the mere existence of human beings attests to the fact that, bordering the world subject to the laws of nature, another world exists that is free of them.

If we look at these things properly, then we have to say that the world we're studying is subject to natural laws, but that bordering it is another world which has nothing to do with these, where other laws prevail. So if we truly immerse ourselves in the dream world, we enter a realm where the laws of nature lose their power. The fact that with their ordinary consciousness people are only able to perceive something fantastic in the dream world is due to the fact that they don't have the ability to understand the context of what they encounter there. It's people who bring fantasticism into it. But what lives and moves there is a completely different world sphere, one in which we're submerged in dreams.

This leads us directly to another point. If we speak to someone who's completely immersed in the conventional wisdom of today, they will say: I study the laws of gravity by observing a falling stone. I can deduce the gravity laws from that. Then I go out into the world and apply these to the stars. This is how they think: here is the earth, where we find natural laws, and there is the universe. They think that the principles they've found on earth also apply to the Orion Nebula or whatever.

Now as we know, gravity is inversely proportional to the square of the separation distance between the two interacting objects and it gets weaker and weaker. Light too decreases with distance and as I've already said the validity of natural laws also decreases. What is valid as a natural law on earth is no longer true out there in the universe. It's only true up to a certain altitude. But out there in the cosmos beyond a certain altitude those laws apply that we find in dreams. Therefore, people should be clear that when we look out to the Orion Nebula, in order to understand it we shouldn't think as we do in experimental physics, rather we should start to dream, as the laws of the Orion Nebula are the principles of dreams.

In fact, human beings used to know something of these things and there are still intimations of this among people who can concentrate in their thinking.

There was a naturalist, who lived not in the second but in the first half of the nineteenth century, and was Haeckel's teacher—Johannes Mueller[44]. He was a person who could really concentrate strongly. He went really deeply into whatever he was studying at the time. By being able to do this, to go deeply into something, we can sometimes understand more. This may also have its dark side as you'll soon see. Johannes Mueller was once asked a question during a summer course he was giving. He answered: 'That's something I only know about in winter, but not in the summer.' In summer he was so strongly concentrated on the subject matter of his summer lectures that he freely admitted to only knowing this answer in winter.

This Johannes Mueller once confessed to something really interesting: he had been dissecting corpses over a long period of time in order to learn more about them. But he doesn't find what he's looking for. However, sometimes he manages to dream about his experiments and then he gains deeper insights, he understands more. This was the first half of the nineteenth century. At that time, you could still allow yourself such extravagances, even if you were a distinguished naturalist.

We human beings enter a completely different world, governed by completely different principles, when we dream. And taking this into account, if we followed Johannes Mueller, we'd not think about the Orion Nebula as they do in the observatories or in the astronomical institutions, but we'd have to dream about it. Then we'd know more than if we just thought about it. I think this is connected to the fact that shepherds used to sleep in the meadows at night and they actually dreamed of the stars and so knew more about them than people of a later age. This is true.

In short, whether we go inside ourselves and approach there the dream world, or out into the universe, we encounter as the ancients would say, beyond the world of the zodiac, the realm of dreams.

Here we come to a point where we can begin to understand what the Greeks, who still knew of such things, meant when they used the word 'chaos'. I've read all sorts of explanations of what chaos is, but I always found that they were far from the truth. What then did the Greeks mean when they spoke of chaos? They meant the principles that we can glimpse when we dream, or that we have to accept at the outermost perimeters of the universe. These principles, which are not those of natural law, the Greeks attributed to chaos. Yes, they said that chaos begins where the laws of nature are no longer existent, where other principles prevail. For the Greeks the world is born out of chaos, which means out of a situation that's not governed by natural laws, but is similar to dreams or to the far reaches of the constellation of Orion and the hunting dogs and so on. Here we come close to a world which is at least heralded in the fantastic but vivid world of dream images.

Now if the physical natural world is here, then we reach a kind of second stream when we submerse ourselves in dreams. Then, however we arrive at a third stream, which lies beyond the realm of dreams and has no direct relationship to natural laws whatsoever. The dream world protests against the laws of nature with its images. As for this third realm, it would be ridiculous to say that it conforms to natural laws in any way. It contradicts completely, even audaciously, the laws of nature, for it is intimately connected to human beings. Whereas dreams appear in the living world of images, this third realm manifests at first in the form of the voice of conscience, in our ethical attitudes.

If we have on the one hand the world of nature and on the other the world of ethics side by side, then there is no overlap. The overlap is in the dream world or in what the experimenter experienced as the world of magic, where the phenomena spoke to him quite differently than did those of the natural world.

Between the world governed by natural law and the world from which our conscience speaks to us, there for our everyday consciousness lies the dream world. However, as here is the waking world, here the dream world and here the world of sleep, this leads us directly to the idea that in actual fact during sleep the gods speak to human beings. This is not a natural process, but an ethical one and when we wake up it manifests as the divine inner voice, as our conscience.

In this way the three worlds come together and we can understand two things: on the one hand why the dream world protests against natural laws and on the other how this dream world overlaps with another world, the reality of which is hidden from everyday consciousness: the world where ethical concepts originate.

If we find our way into this world, then we discover the further reaches of the spiritual world, where natural laws hold no sway, only spiritual ones, whereas in dreams natural and spiritual laws are all mixed up together, because the dream world is a transition between these two realms.

Thus, we've looked from one perspective at how human beings are integrated into these three worlds.

Jakob Boehme, Paracelsus, Swedenborg

DORNACH, 23 SEPTEMBER 1923

Looking at the dream world, as we did yesterday, drew our attention to the fact that when we go from the world, that's spread out before our senses as the world of natural laws, into another world, these laws actually don't apply. I'd say that they stop applying gradually, little by little. In the case of dreams, we notice that on the one side they quite clearly comply up to a point with the laws of nature, but on the other side moral and ethical considerations also play a part in the way things interact with each other, so that these relationships express something like the moral values of the dreamer. Dreams are like a gentle transition from the physical world of the senses to completely different worlds, that have nothing to do with mere laws of nature.

Now it's important that through the ideas and feelings that arise when we direct our soul power towards the transitions we find in dreams, we reach a human understanding of the way things interact in the world, as otherwise this all remains just a closed book. You'll soon see what I mean. Developing intellectual concepts for these things is not really the point. What's important is that we totally appreciate things, that we have a real human relationship with everything we're connected to in our lives and through the fact that we're human beings. And it's impossible to say anything or think anything about certain aspects of life, if we haven't been touched by, haven't felt something of what we spoke about yesterday concerning dreams. It all depends on this tonality of our feelings. This is why I want to add to what I said yesterday about dreams and about the curious statements of the experimental magician something directly related to the phenomena of our lives and which should really be seen as a much greater mystery than is usually the case. In connection with yesterday's lecture, we want to look from a certain perspective at those people who are usually described as 'somnambulists'. These are people who exhibit many anomalies in their lives and even go as far as getting out of bed in the night and climbing around on the roof without falling off.

Secondly, I want to talk from a certain point of view about several individuals, whom we've often spoken of in a different context[45]: Jakob Boehme, Paracelsus and a third person, Swedenborg. We can argue that people of today are quite apathetic; the kind of interests that I would call feuilletonistic are very widespread. Really, such people as the somnambulists, Jakob Boehme or Swedenborg should be like a wake-up call, as they're so different from normal members of the public.

Now let's try to understand these phenomena. We start with the ordinary sleepwalkers. You'll know that in a certain way their activities are connected to the phases of the moon. Just recently—and that's one of the reasons I'm talking about it here—we've spoken of the moon's significance in the universe[46]. I said that there were beings, who were once on the earth and brought humanity primeval truth, which then gradually died away; if we go back far enough in history we can find them. These beings withdrew to a kind of world colony in the moon and now inhabit the inside of the moon. And it's actually the case that in a coarse form a small residual group of these beings have remained on earth. At the time when these moon beings of today were still on earth as the great teachers and leaders of humanity, human beings were very different.

These beings left physical phenomena behind on earth, meaning the facts of reproductive life. The facts of reproductive life in their present form didn't exist on earth at the time when these beings brought humanity primeval truth. It's similar to when you've dissolved some substance in a fluid and the fluid looks quite clean and undisturbed, but when the substance sinks to the bottom then you see the substance is coarse and the fluid is finer than it was before—this is roughly how it is with what I'm describing here. What now exists on earth as reproductive life is coarse by comparison to what it once was. And what these beings took with them into the moon sphere had become infinitely finer and more spiritual. But they both belong together and have been differentiated out of each other. As I said when I was discussing the position of the moon in the cosmos, the influence that the moon still exerts on the earth today is such that it reflects back not just the light of the sun but all that is in the cosmos. In the moon, therefore, we have two things: the inside of the moon, which has closed itself off, doesn't at present appear on the outside and has another task in the world, and then what the moon reflects.

Now in what concerns our physical bodies, we humans are subject to gravity both when we move and when we're just sitting down. Gravity is always present. If our physical bodies weren't subject to it, then we wouldn't be able to assume these various positions such as walking, standing, sitting and so on.

But with our etheric bodies we're not subject to gravity but to the force of the moon. The etheric body is exposed to this force reflected back from the universe and this draws it out. Whereas gravity pulls us down, the force of the moon draws us out into the cosmos. This moon force is active in somnambulist personalities. For a few moments the moon force overcomes gravity and these people then behave as if they only had an etheric body, which follows the moon completely freely. They drag their physical bodies along with them, climb about in the most daredevil manner as only the etheric body can and the physical absolutely can't; but it gets dragged along in those moments in time. So basically, it's an irruption of specific moon forces, which takes place in these somnambulist personalities.

However, now we have to explore further, because all this takes place in the greater context of the world, which in the end consists of beings. All phenomena outside beings are just illusory; in the cosmos only beings are truly real. Truly real are the beings in the mineral realm, in the plant realm and in the animal realm, truly real are human beings, the angels, the archangels and so on. They are realities; individualized beings are realities. The rest is something that goes on between the beings; the rest is appearance and isn't reality. Therefore, when we speak of realities, then we're dealing with beings.

Now the question is, when such beings as somnambulists, who are individualized human beings, appear, how does this phenomenon fit in to the cosmos as a whole? How did it come about that somnambulism exists in the universe?

Now you have to understand what I'm about to say not in a logical, intellectual way, but more in a feeling context as this is the appropriate logic for our subject matter. Try to fill yourself with the feeling of going beyond the world of natural laws and beyond the realm of dreams and out into completely different worlds, where natural law doesn't hold any more and where other relationships prevail. Try to really feel your way into this and then you'll become aware that you could ask: What about those people who appeared in one or another incarnation as somnambulists, what happens to them in the life before birth or after death?

Now you know already that there are dark aspects to this condition including a kind of mediumship and that somnambulists are different from the average citizen. They act differently in their lives, their behaviour is different, in short, they are just different. Now if they're different in earthly life then, if we can actually go beyond the dream realm and its impressions and into the spiritual world, we would have to ask whether they're different from other people in the world bordering the earthly one, in life before birth. What are they like in that world?

You see these beings, who are sleepwalkers in their earthly incarnation, were extremely antagonistic in their pre-earthly existence and behaved in a hostile way towards the spiritual.

If, with the methods we have and which I've often described, you do research into the pre-earthly life of a somnambulist—since the French course[47] we've often spoken quite concretely about this pre-earthly life—then you would ask: what were these somnambulists like before they descended into earthly existence? And regardless of the fact that it might sound preposterous, we have to say that in their pre-earthly lives in the spiritual world they were materialists.

Of course, people aren't materialists there in the sense that they entertain theoretical views about materialism. There we move in a world of sympathy and antipathy and not in a world of concepts and opinions. These sleepwalkers lived in the spiritual world, but most of what they experienced in the spiritual world was disagreeable to them. Whatever they encountered in the spiritual world appeared to them in such a way that they hated it. And because of this, when they descended to earthly existence, they couldn't consolidate their astral body in the right way. When we come down to earthly life, we have to consolidate our astral body. This consolidation is adversely affected by the fact that these beings have continually absorbed forces of antipathy against the spiritual. Consequently, there develops this karma aligned to the cosmos, that though they have a physical body in earthly life, they have to bind themselves to this body in a way that only an astral body which hasn't been consolidated would do.

Now I've described to you how, when we descend to earth again, we pass through the moon sphere and absorb the forces of the moon. These beings have too little independence in relation to the moon forces. They're not sufficiently consolidated in themselves and so they retain a certain affinity with the moon forces when they enter their physical bodies. The consequence is that these people are less considerate of their physical bodies than is the average citizen. They remain subject to the moon sphere, which is a kind of cosmic educational tool to help them to unlearn their hostility towards the spiritual. Thus, with these sleepwalkers we have people who in this life are meant to learn how to break the habit of enmity towards the spiritual. By not fully taking hold of their physical bodies, they experience the spiritual on earth, whereas when they were in the spiritual world, they didn't experience the spiritual enough.

The average person is firmly rooted in their physis; today even more so than is good for humanity we are most firmly fixed in the physical body. But the somnambulists don't really respond to the physical body and therefore, under certain constellations, they're subjected more to the moon forces than to those of the earth.

Now let's move on from these personalities to others such as Jakob Boehme or Paracelsus, who achieved a certain greatness. Historically you could always find such personalities, although less in modern times; but it's not so long ago that there were always what I'd like to call mini Jakob Boehmes. Up until a few decades ago you'd always be able to find such little Jakob Boehmes, these personalities who, if you looked at them from the outside, always stood out because they were able to see into nature more deeply than the average person.

Take a typical phenomenon in the case of Jakob Boehme[48]. In his youth there were already signs of what he would become. Take, for example, the quite typical event that, while he's looking after animals with the others, he suddenly has the urge to leave the herd and the other shepherds and go up into the mountains to a certain place. Guided by instinct he explores a particular place. There he finds a hole, an opening in the earth. He examines it and finds a treasure. It shines up at him. He's deeply affected by it, awestruck, but still he leaves it as it is and goes away. It doesn't occur to him to take anything. Later he often goes back to the place to take another look. However, the hole is no longer there, although the treasure must at least have been buried. He should really have thoroughly convinced himself that what he had seen wasn't actually of the physical world, but being who he was spiritually, he never for a moment thought that he might not have seen anything.

This foreshadows what later emerged as his spirituality: he could see into the essence of things, into what happens at the borders of the spheres. If you read Jakob Boehme's writings with a minimum of understanding you'll notice that this man saw salt or sulphur differently from the average chemist of his times. He writes from a completely different level of insight. He speaks from insights which are unfamiliar even for himself, so that words sometimes don't come near expressing what he sees, the language becomes chaotic and confused and we have to feel our way into it if we want to understand the visions of this Jakob Boehme.

Now to show you this whole phenomenon Jakob Boehme I'd like to remind you of what I've said about the Druids[49]. They used to dampen down the sunlight through their cromlechs and then they looked into the ensuing shadow and saw there the spirituality that radiated from the sun. For other people shadow is just shadow, something negative, an absence of light. But for the Druids it was something quite real. Also, the shadow was not only different according to the time of year, whether it appeared in March or October, but also according to its inner bearing, its colour or tone and also through its spiritual content. If you push back, so to speak, physical sunlight, then what the sun radiates spiritually appears right in the ensuing shadow. With Jakob Boehme this was what happened in his whole human being. He could give himself, so to speak, a push in a certain direction—this is only a rough approximation—and then he could extinguish physical sunlight and see into the darkness.

What happens when you look at something and don't follow the light but have something like a border before you? The result is something like a mirror. But when you look—and although I'm drawing an eye here, it's not really a question of a physical eye—then there's light everywhere. This means we're seeing physical things. But if through our own power we extinguish this physical sunlight, then this looking into darkness appears—we don't even need a shadow. And when this looking into darkness appears then it acts like a mirror. By doing this Jakob Boehme could see how things are reflected in the mirror and to his soul's eye they revealed their inner spiritual content. If he prepared himself, he could see, for example, the most everyday things such as salt, sulphur, mercury and so on, not as we usually see them, but their real being and what lies behind them spiritually, reflected in the darkness.

This was his special vision: he saw reflected in the darkness what lies spiritually behind things. He saw them in the light of the sun's force, whereby the physical effects of light and warmth were excluded. Sleepwalkers connect their will to the forces of the moon and then when for a few moments they're less affected by gravity, are more affected by the moon. Whereas ordinary sleepwalkers follow more the forces of the moon with their organs of will, Boehme could follow the forces of the sun with his organ of cognition, and was therefore a sun person, in a sense sunstruck as opposed to moonstruck. And Jakob Boehme was an outstanding example of such people, human individualities who stand out from the rest of humanity through their special relationship to the spiritual—sun people.

Then again with these sun people we have to ask: what were they like in their pre-earthly existence? Now you see, the pre-earthly existence of such people is extremely interesting. I've often reminded you of how in early phases of human development, people could always look back to their pre-earthly existence: something appeared in their consciousness which made this possible. They knew: I have descended from the spiritual worlds into the earthly world.

What appeared atavistically in Jakob Boehme and Paracelsus was not a personal retrospect, but more a reconnecting to our vision in the spiritual world before earthly existence. Such people relate more to the elemental spirits of nature than to what appears on the surface. They see more the spiritual beings within nature. For example, in pre-earthly existence there is nothing like what we call sulphur on earth, however, there certainly is an elemental spirit which lies behind sulphur. We can perceive this spirit in pre-earthly existence.

Yellow sulphur or any other colour of sulphur—these don't exist in pre-earthly life. Even the idea of this 'sulphur', which people on earth talk about, doesn't exist there. Nothing like this earthly sulphur exists in pre-earthly life, but there is a notion of the spirit, the spiritual essence behind physical sulphur, which is of a very different nature. People like Jakob Boehme and Paracelsus bring this with them.

So they have the power to exclude physical sunlight and—I can't say they can see the spiritual effects of the sun because they aren't visible, just as the light and the colours aren't visible—they push against this physical darkness with their perception, but on a spiritual level, and this then reflects or mirrors the spiritual that exists in the beings and forces of nature.

Normally people pay no attention to the ways in which such impulses appear, but in essence if such people who show the way didn't sometimes live among us, then humanity would know little about nature. People need these inspirations for even the most abstract knowledge of nature. Other people then look after the work of clothing all this in reason. But actually looking into the depths of living nature, that's what these sun people do.

You see the more the nineteenth century developed the more difficult it became to express such things in the world. Most of you will be familiar with the biography of Jakob Boehme. You'll know how he was persecuted. If he or someone like him with this special way of expressing themselves had appeared in the last third of the nineteenth century, they would probably have been locked away in a lunatic asylum. It would have been much worse for him than it was in his own times, even though it was difficult enough back then. At least Jakob Boehme had the benefit at that time of not being maltreated with the likes of what we have to learn in school today. Education, school education hadn't progressed as far as it has today. Now please don't think that I want to say anything against school education, but we have to be able to assess things from another perspective. Probably not many of you grew up where the teacher was, for example, just the retired shoemaker. In such a place the children of those times, and these are the adults of today, didn't learn much in the way of knowledge as they do today; they remained much more innocent. However, what we learn in school today doesn't only cultivate, it also deadens something. Jakob Boehme had the benefit of not being subjected to such an education and so the sun person living inside him could work its way to the surface.

Yes, all this is inside people but sometimes it has to find another way out. In certain compositions from the last third of the nineteenth century I could show you how people, who because they'd gone through the school education system of that time and therefore couldn't speak like Jakob Boehme, expressed all this in musical compositions. There's a basic tone, a prevailing mood similar to that in the writings of Jakob Boehme. At some point it breaks through, especially in music, but not in what is generally acclaimed. Don't think I mean a piece of Wagner's or even *Hansel and Gretel* when talking about these things[50]. I'd have to name some completely different pieces. But there are such musical achievements where something breaks through. And as I've said, it's precisely things like this which are important for earthly life.

Now we can look at the third type of person, who is so well represented by Swedenborg. If we only look at the surface Swedenborg seems very idiosyncratic. He made his way successfully until the middle of his life; in his forties he was recognized as a great scholar of his time and had studied all branches of contemporary science comprehensively. Many of his works have been published. However, there are an enormous number of writings about the science of the day, which only existed until recently in manuscript form. Now a scholarly Swedish society has taken on the task of publishing these works of Swedenborg, which were written in his 40s on the prevailing scientific themes.

But then Swedenborg changes and people start to say that he's gone mad. He's gone completely mad! His works are being published as written by one of the great scholars of the age and not just the efforts of one colleague, but those of a whole academy of colleagues are needed to master the task of making the Swedenborg that existed up until his 40s available to the general public. And the later Swedenborg is of no interest at all! However, it's significant that Swedenborg lived the life of a scholar of his times up until a certain age and then a certain spiritual vision broke through.

Such a spiritual vision as Swedenborg experienced has its special characteristics. It's as follows: normally if you imagine a person and look at their brain, then in a certain sense the etheric body fills out the brain. What I'm drawing here in red [image unavailable] is the physical brain. The etheric body fills out the physical brain and projects out a little bit.

Now up until his 40s Swedenborg had developed his etheric body and his brain, his head constitution, in the normal, I could say, bourgeois way. Then, however, a force overwhelmed him which pulled the etheric body tighter, of course not beneath the skin, but pulled it so tightly together that it became denser and more independent of the brain while he still remained as clever. Because it's not true that he became a foolish man; he was just as intelligent as before.

When someone walks in their sleep, then their astral body is subject to the influence of the moon. Often their organs of will are attuned to the lunar forces. And someone like Jakob Boehme has directed their powers of cognition towards the forces of the sun, pushing back the physical effects of the sun. But with Swedenborg, who had this tightening of the etheric body, it is the force of Saturn at work. It is that force of Saturn which I recently described as cosmic[51], in which lies something akin to the whole inwardness of our planetary system, so that we can say that Saturn contains the forces of memory of our whole solar system. And what passed over to Swedenborg were these forces of Saturn, this inwardness of the whole planetary system. This was why he could see things in the visions he described. He saw angels, archangels and processes going on between angels and archangels just as he describes them. But what was all this really? Where had he landed through this tightening of the head part of the etheric body? He didn't really gain access to processes among the hierarchies. You have to imagine what he saw in the following way: if the earth is here then we can draw the etheric sphere of the earth. This goes out into the cosmic expanses about which I told you yesterday and we arrive at the Orion Nebula and so on, which has its own laws, not natural laws, but laws as they are in dreams. Only when space ends would we arrive at the life of the hierarchies. Swedenborg couldn't see into that with his visionary gift, but all those processes which take place beyond the etheric sphere are not only reflected in the ether, they also evoke actual image processes in the ether. So when something happens up among the hierarchies, which we would have to describe quite differently, it has an effect on the ether sphere of the earth, so that the etheric forms act upon the ether of the earth. Forms are working around us which are not the actual angels, but forms created from the ether, which then transform their actions so that humans can understand them.

Swedenborg could see these actual reflections, as we can call them, of the higher hierarchies in the earth's ether. Thus, he didn't actually see what the angels did, but he saw what becomes visible when their deeds are reflected in the earth's ether in the human sphere. The deeds of the angels up there can't directly work on earthly human beings, but these actual reflections affect humanity. The etheric reflections circulate among human beings and work on them. This is what Swedenborg noticed and could see in the ether.

Whereas with moonstruck people we're prompted to look at their pre-earthly existence and with Jakob Boehme or Paracelsus at their earthly lives, with someone like Swedenborg it's his existence after death. His earthly life only makes sense when we look at his existence after death. For it's such people especially, who after death are able to teach others, who have also passed through the gates of death, and to explain many things, which in the higher worlds would otherwise remain unintelligible to someone who hasn't acquired any knowledge of the spiritual worlds during their earthly life.

It's part of the general spiritual world-plan that human personalities such as Swedenborg are initiated into these reflections, the mirror images of the processes of the higher hierarchies, so that they are well-prepared for life after death, where they will need it. Whereas the earthly existence of the somnambulists is akin to a reform school with regard to the spiritual worlds, the life of someone like Swedenborg has the character of a preparation for what they will have to achieve after death. So we can say, that human beings are diverse in their individualities and those who are at the extremes show us how we can only understand humans, when we not only study their relationship to their earthly environment, but when we realize that in every moment of their lives here on earth, people also have a relationship to the spiritual worlds. All that happens to people here in their earthly lives, especially to people like Boehme and the others, who have such unusual experiences, is related to pre-earthly existence, to the spirit that also lives in earthly existence, or to life after death. We only notice clearly in the case of sleepwalkers or of someone like Jakob Boehme or Swedenborg something that is true up to a point for all human beings—the orientation of earthly life towards pre-earthly or post-earthly spiritual existence, or towards the spiritual during earthly life. In particular it's those beings, who act in the cosmos as I've described here, the moon beings, the sun beings and the Saturn beings, who need the powers which such special people have for their activities.

Then we can begin to discern a new perspective, which I just want to mention in conclusion. What this opens up is something I want to talk about in the next lecture here[52]. In this perspective we have to consider that the human interior, even the physical interior inside the skin, is actually quite different from the rest of what we call the cosmos.

Just to describe this roughly: if we have the earth here, then mineral, vegetable, animal and physical-human processes and so on take place on it—things happen that we can perceive with our senses and understand with our minds. Here are the human beings on the earth. But on the inside of human beings there is also a whole world that's not the same as the outside world. I could, for example, sketch human beings but only their insides. What happens inside humans is here in red and the white all around is the natural world we can see with our senses and so on. Now we can make an abstraction. Just imagine I'm deleting all these natural forces and just leaving the red; this means I'm deleting everything except the human interior. Now imagine that here on earth I'd remove first all the minerals, then all the plants, all the animals and everything else that was in some way a force of nature. And then not only all the skin, so that the physical skin has gone, but all the physical matter that humans have in them. I take all that away, but still there's something left of the earthly sphere: the divine forces. We'd still have the hierarchies, the angels, archangels and so on. In reality we would have taken away the earth but retained the heavens.

Now if you follow this idea, then you'll find a way to position the human interior in relation to the spiritual super-sensible world, so that you can imagine in a more comprehensive way where the heavens are. They are actually inside human beings, in what is left after we've taken all that away, as I've just said.

Now if we describe as I did today people like the somnambulists, Jakob Boehme or Swedenborg, what are we really talking about? Then we're not standing on the earth but are standing in the cosmos. That's what's needed in our times, that we don't just talk about human beings in general terms as they did in the last few centuries, as if they were only a conglomeration of external natural forces and effects. Today we have to pay attention to what's left over if we take all that away. I don't want to repeat that gruesome description, but what is left over after we've taken away everything else and just left the inside of the human being. Then we'd be left with the spiritual world, not only in an abstract, pantheistic way, but with the concrete spiritual world of super-sensible beings. They dwell in human beings. We humans have to become aware again of the fact that the human body is the dwelling place of the gods.

Only when this has become a part of our contemporary consciousness, will it be the necessary impulse for the rise of civilization instead of its decline. This is a truth that I could express from many different perspectives. Today I did so by relating it to what I said yesterday about dreams and earlier about abnormal soul states.

NOTES

Works of Rudolf Steiner that are part of the Collected Works are referred to in these notes with their bibliography (GA) numbers. See also the summary at the end of this volume.

[1] Before the lecture Rudolf Steiner reported briefly on his trip to Prague from 26 April to 1 May 1923 and the lectures he gave there. He said: 'I just want to tell you briefly about the Prague trip. It was organized so that I was to give two public lectures and two branch lectures. The public lectures were very well-attended. The first took place in the local scientific institute "Urania". The eurythmy performance took place on Sunday as a matinee in the sizeable Deutsches Theater in Prague in front of a capacity audience.

'On this occasion we could really see how great the longing is for a spiritual life, for the renewal of spiritual life, and that it's just a question of finding a way to those many people who today are seeking such a renewal of spiritual life. There are many such people as we saw in this case, a great many such people in the world today in every nation.

'Unfortunately, Marie Steiner couldn't do the recitation as she was indisposed and she can't do those for the eurythmy performances in Breslau, Nuremberg and Heidenheim which follow those in Prague and Stuttgart.'

[2] *In the penultimate issue of* The Goetheanum: See the essay 'Anthroposophy and Idealism' in 'The idea of the Goetheanum in the midst of the contemporary cultural crisis. Collected essays from the periodical *The Goetheanum* 1921-1925', GA36.

[3] *Swabian Vischer*. Friedrich Theodor Vischer (1807-1887), aesthetician and poet. His works mentioned here: *Auch Einer* ('One Too') (1879), *Faust. Part three of the tragedy*, (a parody, 1862), *Fashion and Cynicism* (1879).

[4] *Ferdinand Keller*, 1800-1881, Switzerland. Archaeologist. In 1853/54 he discovered the lake dwellings in Obermeilen on Lake Zurich.

[5] *Gottfried Semper*, 1803-1879, well-known architect. Main work is *Style in the Technical and Tectonic Arts* (1860-1863).

[6] *in the penultimate issue of* The Goetheanum: see note 2.

[7] *Bim, Bam, Bum*. From the *Galgenlieder* by Christian Morgenstern.

[8] *'the lectures on cosmology, religion and philosophy'*: GA 215

[9] *'Jehovah tormented someone in their sleep in relation to their kidneys'*: Psalm 73, verses 20-21. Translator's note: in the modern English versions of this psalm the kidneys don't appear.

[10] *'our remedy'*: *'Infludo'*, made by Weleda AG, Arlesheim/Switzerland and Schwaebisch-Gmuend/Germany.

[11] *'as was described by Leinhas in the recent* Goetheanum': Emil Leinhas, 'Socialization or association?' in *The Goetheanum*, Volume 2, 1922/1923, Nr. 37, 22nd April 1923.

[12] After the lecture Rudolf Steiner said: 'Now, my dear friends, to compensate for the fact that I wasn't here on Friday and I can't be here again until Whitsun, I'd like to give another lecture tomorrow before I leave. So, tomorrow morning at 8am I'll continue with these reflections.' This lecture announced for the 7 May 1923 is published in the volume 'The Human Soul and its Connection with the Divine-Spiritual Individuals. The Internalization of the Festivals of the Year.' GA224

[13] *'where I spoke about a newly published text'*: About *The Decay and Restoration of Civilization* by Albert Schweitzer. The first part is in the essay 'Real and apparent cultural perspectives' Bern 1923, and in 'The idea of the Goetheanum in the midst of the contemporary cultural crisis. Collected essays from the periodical *The Goetheanum* 1921-1925', GA36.

[14] *'in the educational lectures yesterday and today'*: 'Why do we need Waldorf education?' in 'Anthroposophical Knowledge of the Human Being and Pedagogy', *Waldorf Education*, Vol. 2, GA 304a.

[15] *'inaugural speech'*: Max Rubner, 'Our goals for the future'. Speech on the occasion of his inauguration as chancellor of the Koenigliche Friedrich-Wilhelm University in Berlin in the assembly hall on 15 October 1910, Leipzig 1910.

[16] Eduard Zeller, 1814-1908. Theologian and historian of philosophy.

[17] *Albert Schweitzer... 'The Decay and Restoration of Civilization'*. Published by Paul Haupt. Academic Bookshop. Formerly Max Drechsel, Bern, 1923. A copy of this edition can be found in Rudolf Steiner's library and is heavily annotated.

[18] *'criticized in a public lecture'*: see lecture on 10 April 1921 in Dornach, GA 76.

[19] *'and now he quotes this historian of philosophy'*: Wilhelm Windelband, 1848-1915. Historian of philosophy. His *History of Philosophy* was published in German in 1891. The passage cited by Schweitzer is on page 564 of the 4th edition, published in German in 1907.

20 *'no mention of Bismarck'*: this couldn't be confirmed.

21 *'general assembly'*: annual general meeting of the Goetheanum Society on 17 June in Dornach.

22 *'This morning in the lecture on education'*: see note 14.

23 *'one news item reports'*: this couldn't be confirmed.

24 *'the nonsense'*: Steiner speaks of 'galamatias', meaning senseless, muddleheaded talk.

25 *George Sand* 1804-1876, real name Aurore Dupin, married name Baroness Dudevant. French author. *The Journeyman Joiner or the Companion of the Tour of France*, Paris 1840.

26 *'simple book'*: by Agricol Perdiguer, known as Avignonnais le vertu. Carpenter who became a member of the 'Gavots' in 1823. His first book, *Devoirs de la Liberté. Chansons de Compagnons* appeared in 1834 and was distributed free of charge to members of the society. George Sand based her novel on his book, *La Livre de Compagnonnage*, Paris, 1839.

27 *'In the latest issue of the journal* Knowledge and Life': July issue of the year 1922/1923.

28 *Nikolai Nikolayevich Strakhov,* 1828-1896, Russian author and philosopher, Hegelian.

29 *'in the issue of* The Goetheanum *that has just appeared'*: in the essays: 'A perhaps topical personal memory'/ 'How today the present transforms itself rapidly into history' / 'The necessary transformation of contemporary spiritual life' / The spirit of yesteryear and the spirit of today' in 'The idea of the Goetheanum in the midst of the contemporary cultural crisis', GA 36.

30 *'Last autumn I gave a course on the world economy'*: 'World Economy' (14 lectures in Dornach from 24 July to 6 August 1922), GA 340.

31 *'homeless souls, a description I used here just a short while ago'*: in 'The Anthroposophic Movement' (8 lectures in Dornach from 10 to 17 June 1923), GA 258.

32 *'As I've mentioned before'*: in the lecture on 29 September 1922 in 'The Fundamental Impulse of the World-Historical Development of Humanity', (8 lectures in Dornach from 16 September to 1 October 1922), GA 216.

33 *'in these four articles'*: see note 29 .

34 *'a little book about botany from the perspective of spiritual science'*: Dr. A. Usteri, 'An Attempt at an Introduction to Botany from a Spiritual Scientific Perspective', Zurich, 1923.

35 *'Here too there has been talk of psychoanalysis'*: particularly in the 2 lectures 'Anthroposophy and Psychoanalysis' held in Dornach on 10 and 11 November 1917 in 'Individual Spiritual Beings and their Influence in the Souls of Human Beings', GA 178.

[36] *Quote from Karl Rosenkranz*: from his diary: Koenigsberg, autumn 1833 to spring 1846; Leipzig, 1854.

[37] *Hamerling … in the* Homunculus: Robert Hamerling (1830-1889). His *Homunculus—a modern epic in ten cantos* was published in 1888. See also the lecture 'Homunculus' held in Berlin on 26 March 1914, in 'Spiritual Science as a Treasure for Life', GA 63.

[38] *'Eduard von Hartmann'*, 1842-1906. 'Philosophy of the Unconscious', 1869. See also Rudolf Steiner, *The Story of My Life* (1923-1925), GA 28.

[39] *An Attempt to Interpret the Metamorphosis of Plants*. See *Goethe's Natural Scientific Writings* with an introduction and commentaries by Rudolf Steiner, published in Kuerschners *German National Literature* (1884-1897), 5 volumes, reprint Dornach 1975, GA 1a-e, volume 1.

[40] *'One philosopher'*: Eduard von Hartmann.

[41] *'when I was visiting'*: in August 1889.

[42] *'The Seeress of Prevorst'*: Justinus Kerner, 1786-1862, poet and attending physician to Friederike Hauffe, a somnambulist, whom he wrote about in his novel *The Seeress of Prevorst*, Stuttgart, 1829.

[43] *Ludwig Staudenmaier's book: Magic as an Experimental Science*, Leipzig, 1912.

[44] *Johannes Mueller*, 1801-1858, physiologist, pathologist and anatomist. Professor in Bonn and later in Berlin. One of the most distinguished medical scientists of his times.

[45] *'often spoken of in a different context'*: cf. lecture on 8 January 1917 in 'Contemporary-historical examinations: The karma of Untruthfulness', GA 174; lecture on 15 April 1921 in 'Materialistic and the Task of Anthroposophy', GA 204; lecture on 3 January 1923 in 'Origins of Natural Science', GA 326.

[46] *'we've spoken of the moon's significance in the universe'*: lecture on 27 July 1923 in 'Initiation Science', GA 228.

[47] *'since the French course'*: see note 8

[48] *'a typical phenomenon in the case of Jakob Boehme'*: Jakob Boehme (1575-1624) didn't write an autobiography. He told Abraham von Franckenberg the story of his life, who then related the following story in his description of Boehme's life:
'Being now grown up a pretty big Lad, he, in Company with the other Boys of the same Village, was obliged to tend the Cattle in the Fields, and in this Way to be serviceable, under due Subjection, to his Parents.
'During the Time of his being a Herd's-Boy, he met with a curious and remarkable Occurrence. Having one Day, about Noon, been rambling to a great Distance from the other Lads, and climbing up alone by himself on the adjacent Mountain, called Land's Crown; being arrived at the Summit, (the Story I have heard

from his own Mouth, and he has pointed me to the Place) he espied amongst the great red Stones a Kind of Aperture or Entrance, over-grown with Bushes, and inclosed in a Manner not much unlike that of a Door-Case, or Passage. This, in his Simplicity, he penetrated into, and there descried a large portable Vessel, or wooden Pannier, full of Money; the Sight of which set him into a Shudder. *This* also prevented his meddling with any of the Money, and put him upon making the very best of his Way out again, without taking so much as a single Piece along with him.

'And what is very remarkable, tho' he had frequently climbed up to the same Place afterwards, in Company of the other Herd's-Boys, yet he could never hit upon this Aperture again. To me it appears, that it might be a Sort of emblematic Omen, or Presage of his future spiritual Admission to the Sight of the hidden Treasury of the Wisdom and Mysteries of God and Nature. This very Treasure, by JACOB's Account, was some Years afterwards carried off by a Foreign Virtuoso; but it brought this Treasure-Hunter to a shameful End, there having been a Curse annexed to it.'

The Life and Death of Jakob Behmen by Abraham von Franckenberg. Translated by Francis Okely. 1780

[49] *'what I've said about the Druids'*: lecture on 10 September 1923, 'The Sun-Initiation of the Druid Priest and his Moon Science' in 'Initiation Science', GA 228.

[50] *'Hansel and Gretel'*: opera of a fairy-tale by Engelbert Humperdinck, 1854-1921, which premiered in Weimar in 1893.

[51] *'that force of Saturn which I recently described as cosmic'*: see note 8 as well as the lecture on 3 January 1923 in 'Origins of Natural Science', GA 326.

[52] *'the next lecture here'*: see lectures on 5, 6, 7, 12 and 13 October 1923, in 'The Four Seasons and the Archangels', GA 229.

Rudolf Steiner's Collected Works

T HE German Edition of Rudolf Steiner's Collected Works (the *Gesamtausgabe* [GA] published by Rudolf Steiner Verlag, Dornach, Switzerland) presently runs to 354 titles, organized either by type of work (written or spoken), chronology, audience (public or other), or subject (education, art, etc.). For ease of comparison, the Collected Works in English [CW] follows the German organization exactly. A complete listing of the CWs follows with literal translations of the German titles. Other than in the case of the books published in his lifetime, titles were rarely given by Rudolf Steiner himself, and were often provided by the editors of the German editions. The titles in English are not necessarily the same as the German; and, indeed, over the past seventy-five years have frequently been different, with the same book sometimes appearing under different titles.

For ease of identification and to avoid confusion, we suggest that readers looking for a title should do so by CW number. Because the work of creating the Collected Works of Rudolf Steiner is an ongoing process, with new titles being published every year, we have not indicated in this listing which books are presently available. To find out what titles in the Collected Works are currently in print, please check our website at www.rudolfsteinerpress.com (or www.steinerbooks.org for US readers).

Written Work

CW 1   Goethe: Natural-Scientific Writings, Introduction, with Footnotes and Explanations in the text by Rudolf Steiner

CW 2   Outlines of an Epistemology of the Goethean World View, with Special Consideration of Schiller

CW 3   Truth and Science

CW 4   The Philosophy of Freedom

CW 4a   Documents to 'The Philosophy of Freedom'

CW 5   Friedrich Nietzsche, A Fighter against His Time

CW 6　Goethe's Worldview

CW 6a　Now in CW 30

CW 7　Mysticism at the Dawn of Modern Spiritual Life and Its Relationship with Modern Worldviews

CW 8　Christianity as Mystical Fact and the Mysteries of Antiquity

CW 9　Theosophy: An Introduction into Supersensible World Knowledge and Human Purpose

CW 10　How Does One Attain Knowledge of Higher Worlds?

CW 11　From the Akasha-Chronicle

CW 12　Levels of Higher Knowledge

CW 13　Occult Science in Outline

CW 14　Four Mystery Dramas

CW 15　The Spiritual Guidance of the Individual and Humanity

CW 16　A Way to Human Self-Knowledge: Eight Meditations

CW 17　The Threshold of the Spiritual World. Aphoristic Comments

CW 18　The Riddles of Philosophy in Their History, Presented as an Outline

CW 19　Contained in CW 24

CW 20　The Riddles of the Human Being: Articulated and Unarticulated in the Thinking, Views and Opinions of a Series of German and Austrian Personalities

CW 21　The Riddles of the Soul

CW 22　Goethe's Spiritual Nature and its Revelation in 'Faust' and through the 'Fairy Tale of the Snake and the Lily'

CW 23　The Central Points of the Social Question in the Necessities of Life in the Present and the Future

CW 24　Essays Concerning the Threefold Division of the Social Organism and the Period 1915-1921

CW 25　Cosmology, Religion and Philosophy

CW 26　Anthroposophical Leading Thoughts

CW 27　Fundamentals for Expansion of the Art of Healing according to Spiritual-Scientific Insights

CW28　The Course of My Life

CW 29　Collected Essays on Dramaturgy, 1889-1900

CW 30　Methodical Foundations of Anthroposophy: Collected Essays on Philosophy, Natural Science, Aesthetics and Psychology, 1884-1901

CW 31　Collected Essays on Culture and Current Events, 1887-1901

CW 32　Collected Essays on Literature, 1884-1902

CW 33　Biographies and Biographical Sketches, 1894-1905

CW 34　Lucifer-Gnosis: Foundational Essays on Anthroposophy and Reports from the Periodicals 'Lucifer' and 'Lucifer-Gnosis,' 1903-1908

CW 35　Philosophy and Anthroposophy: Collected Essays, 1904-1923

CW 36　The Goetheanum-Idea in the Middle of the Cultural Crisis of the Present: Collected Essays from the Periodical 'Das Goetheanum,' 1921-1925

Public Lectures

Lectures to the Members of the Anthroposophical Society

SIGNIFICANT EVENTS IN THE LIFE OF
RUDOLF STEINER

1829:   June 23: birth of Johann Steiner (1829–1910)—Rudolf Steiner's father—in Geras, Lower Austria.

1834:   May 8: birth of Franciska Blie (1834–1918)—Rudolf Steiner's mother—in Horn, Lower Austria. 'My father and mother were both children of the glorious Lower Austrian forest district north of the Danube.'

1860:   May 16: marriage of Johann Steiner and Franciska Blie.

1861:   February 25: birth of *Rudolf Joseph Lorenz Steiner* in Kraljevec, Croatia, near the border with Hungary, where Johann Steiner works as a telegrapher for the South Austria Railroad. Rudolf Steiner is baptized two days later, February 27, the date usually given as his birthday.

1862:   Summer: the family moves to Modling, Lower Austria.

1863:   The family moves to Pottschach, Lower Austria, near the Styrian border, where Johann Steiner becomes station master. 'The view stretched to the mountains . . . majestic peaks in the distance and the sweet charm of nature in the immediate surroundings.'

1864:   November 15: birth of Rudolf Steiner's sister, Leopoldine (d. November 1, 1927). She will become a seamstress and live with her parents for the rest of her life.

1866:   July 28: birth of Rudolf Steiner's deaf-mute brother, Gustav (d. May 1, 1941).

1867:   Rudolf Steiner enters the village school. Following a disagreement between his father and the schoolmaster, whose wife falsely accused the boy of causing a commotion, Rudolf Steiner is taken out of school and taught at home.

1868:   A critical experience. Unknown to the family, an aunt dies in a distant town. Sitting in the station waiting room, Rudolf Steiner sees her 'form,' which speaks to him, asking for help. 'Beginning with this experience, a new soul life began in the boy, one in which not only the outer trees and mountains spoke to him, but also the worlds that lay behind them. From this moment on, the boy began to live with the spirits of nature . . .'

1869:   The family moves to the peaceful, rural village of Neudorfl, near Wiener Neustadt in present-day Austria. Rudolf Steiner attends the village school. Because of the 'unorthodoxy' of his writing and spelling, he has to do 'extra lessons'.

1870:   Through a book lent to him by his tutor, he discovers geometry: 'To grasp something purely in the spirit brought me inner happiness. I know that I first learned happiness through geometry.' The same tutor allows him to draw, while other students still struggle with their reading and writing. 'An artistic element' thus enters his education.

1871:   Though his parents are not religious, Rudolf Steiner becomes a 'church child,' a favourite of the priest, who was 'an exceptional character.' 'Up to the age of ten or eleven, among those I came to know, he was far and away the most significant.' Among other things, he introduces Steiner to Copernican, heliocentric cosmology. As an altar boy, Rudolf Steiner serves at masses, funerals, and Corpus Christi processions. At year's end, after an incident in which he escapes a thrashing, his father forbids him to go to church.

1872:   Rudolf Steiner transfers to grammar school in Wiener-Neustadt, a five-mile walk from home, which must be done in all weathers.

1873–75:   Through his teachers and on his own, Rudolf Steiner has many wonderful experiences with science and mathematics. Outside school, he teaches himself analytic geometry, trigonometry, differential equations, and calculus.

1876:   Rudolf Steiner begins tutoring other students. He learns bookbinding from his father. He also teaches himself stenography.

1877:   Rudolf Steiner discovers Kant's *Critique of Pure Reason,* which he reads and rereads. He also discovers and reads von Rotteck's *World History.*

1878:   He studies extensively in contemporary psychology and philosophy.

1879:   Rudolf Steiner graduates from high school with honours. His father is transferred to Inzersdorf, near Vienna. He uses his first visit to Vienna 'to purchase a great number of philosophy books'—Kant, Fichte, Schelling, and Hegel, as well as numerous histories of philosophy. His aim: to find a path from the 'I' to nature.

October
1879–1883: Rudolf Steiner attends the Technical College in Vienna—to study mathematics, chemistry, physics, mineralogy, botany, zoology,

biology, geology, and mechanics—with a scholarship. He also attends lectures in history and literature, while avidly reading philosophy on his own. His two favourite professors are Karl Julius Schröer (German language and literature) and Edmund Reitlinger (physics). He also audits lectures by Robert Zimmermann on aesthetics and Franz Brentano on philosophy. During this year he begins his friendship with Moritz Zitter (1861–1921), who will help support him financially when he is in Berlin.

1880: Rudolf Steiner attends lectures on Schiller and Goethe by Karl Julius Schröer, who becomes his mentor. Also 'through a remarkable combination of circumstances,' he meets Felix Koguzki, a 'herb gatherer' and healer, who could 'see deeply into the secrets of nature'. Rudolf Steiner will meet and study with this 'emissary of the Master' throughout his time in Vienna.

1881: January: '... I didn't sleep a wink. I was busy with philosophical problems until about 12:30 a.m. Then, finally, I threw myself down on my couch. All my striving during the previous year had been to research whether the following statement by Schelling was true or not: *Within everyone dwells a secret, marvellous capacity to draw back from the stream of time—out of the self clothed in all that comes to us from outside—into our innermost being and there, in the immutable form of the Eternal, to look into ourselves.* I believe, and I am still quite certain of it, that I discovered this capacity in myself; I had long had an inkling of it. Now the whole of idealist philosophy stood before me in modified form. What's a sleepless night compared to that!'

Rudolf Steiner begins communicating with leading thinkers of the day, who send him books in return, which he reads eagerly.

July: 'I am not one of those who dives into the day like an animal in human form. I pursue a quite specific goal, an idealistic aim— knowledge of the truth! This cannot be done offhandedly. It requires the greatest striving in the world, free of all egotism, and equally of all resignation.'

August: Steiner puts down on paper for the first time thoughts for a 'Philosophy of Freedom.' 'The striving for the absolute: this human yearning is freedom.' He also seeks to outline a 'peasant philosophy,' describing what the worldview of a 'peasant'—one who lives close to the earth and the old ways—really is.

1881–1882: Felix Koguzki, the herb gatherer, reveals himself to be the envoy of another, higher initiatory personality, who instructs Rudolf Steiner to penetrate Fichte's philosophy and to master modern scientific thinking as a preparation for right entry into the spirit. This 'Master' also teaches him the double (evolutionary and involutionary) nature of time.

1882: Through the offices of Karl Julius Schröer, Rudolf Steiner is asked by Joseph Kürschner to edit Goethe's scientific works for the *Deutschen National-Literatur* edition. He writes 'A Possible Critique of Atomistic Concepts' and sends it to Friedrich Theodor Vischer.

1883: Rudolf Steiner completes his college studies and begins work on the Goethe project.

1884: First volume of Goethe's *Scientific Writings* (CW 1) appears (March). He lectures on Goethe and Lessing, and Goethe's approach to science. In July, he enters the household of Ladislaus and Pauline Specht as tutor to the four Specht boys. He will live there until 1890. At this time, he meets Josef Breuer (1842–1925), the co-author with Sigmund Freud of *Studies in Hysteria,* who is the Specht family doctor.

1885: While continuing to edit Goethe's writings, Rudolf Steiner reads deeply in contemporary philosophy (Eduard von Hartmann, Johannes Volkelt, and Richard Wahle, among others).

1886: May: Rudolf Steiner sends Kürschner the manuscript of *Outlines of Goethe's Theory of Knowledge* (CW 2), which appears in October, and which he sends out widely. He also meets the poet Marie Eugenie Delle Grazie and writes 'Nature and Our Ideals' for her. He attends her salon, where he meets many priests, theologians, and philosophers, who will become his friends. Meanwhile, the director of the Goethe Archive in Weimar requests his collaboration with the *Sophien* edition of Goethe's works, particularly the writings on colour.

1887: At the beginning of the year, Rudolf Steiner is very sick. As the year progresses and his health improves, he becomes increasingly 'a man of letters,' lecturing, writing essays, and taking part in Austrian cultural life. In August–September, the second volume of Goethe's *Scientific Writings* appears.

1888: January–July: Rudolf Steiner assumes editorship of the 'German Weekly' *(Deutsche Wochenschrift)*. He begins lecturing more intensively, giving, for example, a lecture titled 'Goethe as Father of a New Aesthetics.' He meets and becomes soul friends with Friedrich Eckstein (1861–1939), a vegetarian, philosopher of symbolism, alchemist, and musician, who will introduce him to various spiritual currents (including Theosophy) and with whom he will meditate and interpret esoteric and alchemical texts.

1889: Rudolf Steiner first reads Nietzsche *(Beyond Good and Evil)*. He encounters Theosophy again and learns of Madame Blavatsky in the theosophical circle around Marie Lang (1858–1934). Here he also meets well-known figures of Austrian life, as well as esoteric figures like the occultist Franz Hartmann and Karl Leinigen-Billigen (translator of C.G. Harrison's *The Transcendental Universe*). During this period, Steiner first reads A.P. Sinnett's *Esoteric Buddhism* and Mabel Collins's *Light on the Path*. He also begins travelling, visiting Budapest, Weimar, and Berlin (where he meets philosopher Eduard von Hartmann).

1890:   Rudolf Steiner finishes Volume 3 of Goethe's scientific writings. He begins his doctoral dissertation, which will become *Truth and Science* (CW 3). He also meets the poet and feminist Rosa Mayreder (1858–1938), with whom he can exchange his most intimate thoughts. In September, Rudolf Steiner moves to Weimar to work in the Goethe-Schiller Archive.

1891:   Volume 3 of the Kürschner edition of Goethe appears. Meanwhile, Rudolf Steiner edits Goethe's studies in mineralogy and scientific writings for the *Sophien* edition. He meets Ludwig Laistner of the Cotta Publishing Company, who asks for a book on the basic question of metaphysics. From this will result, ultimately, *The Philosophy of Freedom* (CW 4), which will be published not by Cotta but by Emil Felber. In October, Rudolf Steiner takes the oral exam for a doctorate in philosophy, mathematics, and mechanics at Rostock University, receiving his doctorate on the twenty-sixth. In November, he gives his first lecture on Goethe's 'Fairy Tale' in Vienna.

1892:   Rudolf Steiner continues work at the Goethe-Schiller Archive and on his *Philosophy of Freedom*. *Truth and Science,* his doctoral dissertation, is published. Steiner undertakes to write Introductions to books on Schopenhauer and Jean Paul for Cotta. At year's end, he finds lodging with Anna Eunike, née Schulz (1853–1911), a widow with four daughters and a son. He also develops a friendship with Otto Erich Hartleben (1864–1905) with whom he shares literary interests.

1893:   Rudolf Steiner begins his habit of producing many reviews and articles. In March, he gives a lecture titled 'Hypnotism, with Reference to Spiritism.' In September, volume 4 of the Kürschner edition is completed. In November, *The Philosophy of Freedom* appears. This year, too, he meets John Henry Mackay (1864–1933), the anarchist, and Max Stirner, a scholar and biographer.

1894:   Rudolf Steiner meets Elisabeth Fürster Nietzsche, the philosopher's sister, and begins to read Nietzsche in earnest, beginning with the as yet unpublished *Antichrist*. He also meets Ernst Haeckel (1834–1919). In the fall, he begins to write *Nietzsche, A Fighter against His Time* (CW 5).

1895:   May, *Nietzsche, A Fighter against His Time* appears.

1896:   January 22: Rudolf Steiner sees Friedrich Nietzsche for the first and only time. Moves between the Nietzsche and the Goethe-Schiller

Archives, where he completes his work before year's end. He falls out with Elisabeth Förster Nietzsche, thus ending his association with the Nietzsche Archive.

1897:   Rudolf Steiner finishes the manuscript of *Goethe's Worldview* (CW 6). He moves to Berlin with Anna Eunike and begins editorship of the *Magazin für Literatur.* From now on, Steiner will write countless reviews, literary and philosophical articles, and so on. He begins lecturing at the 'Free Literary Society.' In September, he attends the Zionist Congress in Basel. He sides with Dreyfus in the Dreyfus affair.

1898:   Rudolf Steiner is very active as an editor in the political, artistic, and theatrical life of Berlin. He becomes friendly with John Henry Mackay and poet Ludwig Jacobowski (1868–1900). He joins Jacobowski's circle of writers, artists, and scientists—'The Coming Ones' *(Die Kommenden)*—and contributes lectures to the group until 1903. He also lectures at the 'League for College Pedagogy.' He writes an article for Goethe's sesquicentennial, 'Goethe's Secret Revelation,' on the 'Fairy Tale of the Green Snake and the Beautiful Lily.'

1898–99:   'This was a trying time for my soul as I looked at Christianity. . . . I was able to progress only by contemplating, by means of spiritual perception, the evolution of Christianity. . . . Conscious knowledge of real Christianity began to dawn in me around the turn of the century. This seed continued to develop. My soul trial occurred shortly before the beginning of the twentieth century. It was decisive for my soul's development that I stood spiritually before the Mystery of Golgotha in a deep and solemn celebration of knowledge.'

1899:   Rudolf Steiner begins teaching and giving lectures and lecture cycles at the Workers' College, founded by Wilhelm Liebknecht (1826–1900). He will continue to do so until 1904. Writes: *Literature and Spiritual Life in the Nineteenth Century; Individualism in Philosophy; Haeckel and His Opponents; Poetry in the Present;* and begins what will become (fifteen years later) *The Riddles of Philosophy* (CW 18). He also meets many artists and writers, including Kothe Kollwitz, Stefan Zweig, and Rainer Maria Rilke. On October 31, he marries Anna Eunike.

1900:   'I thought that the turn of the century must bring humanity a new light. It seemed to me that the separation of human thinking and willing from the spirit had peaked. A turn or reversal of direction in human evolution seemed to me a necessity.' Rudolf Steiner finishes *World and Life Views in the Nineteenth Century* (the second part of what will become *The Riddles of Philosophy*) and dedicates it to

Ernst Haeckel. It is published in March. He continues lecturing at *Die Kommenden,* whose leadership he assumes after the death of Jacobowski. Also, he gives the Gutenberg Jubilee lecture before 7,000 typesetters and printers. In September, Rudolf Steiner is invited by Count and Countess Brockdorff to lecture in the Theosophical Library. His first lecture is on Nietzsche. His second lecture is titled 'Goethe's Secret Revelation.' October 6, he begins a lecture cycle on the mystics that will become *Mystics after Modernism* (CW 7). November–December: 'Marie von Sivers appears in the audience. . . .' Also in November, Steiner gives his first lecture at the Giordano Bruno Bund (where he will continue to lecture until May, 1905). He speaks on Bruno and modern Rome, focusing on the importance of the philosophy of Thomas Aquinas as monism.

1901: In continual financial straits, Rudolf Steiner's early friends Moritz Zitter and Rosa Mayreder help support him. In October, he begins the lecture cycle *Christianity as Mystical Fact* (CW 8) at the Theosophical Library. In November, he gives his first 'theosophical lecture' on Goethe's 'Fairy Tale' in Hamburg at the invitation of Wilhelm Hubbe-Schleiden. He also attends a gathering to celebrate the founding of the Theosophical Society at Count and Countess Brockdorff's. He gives a lecture cycle, 'From Buddha to Christ,' for the circle of the *Kommenden.* November 17, Marie von Sivers asks Rudolf Steiner if Theosophy needs a Western–Christian spiritual movement (to complement Theosophy's Eastern emphasis). 'The question was posed. Now, following spiritual laws, I could begin to give an answer. . . .' In December, Rudolf Steiner writes his first article for a theosophical publication. At year's end, the Brockdorffs and possibly Wilhelm Hubbe-Schleiden ask Rudolf Steiner to join the Theosophical Society and undertake the leadership of the German section. Rudolf Steiner agrees, on the condition that Marie von Sivers (then in Italy) work with him.

1902: Beginning in January, Rudolf Steiner attends the opening of the Workers' School in Spandau with Rosa Luxemberg (1870–1919). January 17, Rudolf Steiner joins the Theosophical Society. In April, he is asked to become general secretary of the German Section of the theosophical Society, and works on preparations for its founding. In July, he visits London for a theosophical congress. He meets Bertram Keightly, G.R.S. Mead, A.P. Sinnett, and Annie Besant, among others. In September, *Christianity as Mystical Fact* appears. In October, Rudolf Steiner gives his first public lecture on Theosophy ('Monism and Theosophy') to about three hundred people at the Giordano Bruno Bund. On October 19–21, the

German Section of the Theosophical Society has its first meeting; Rudolf Steiner is the general secretary, and Annie Besant attends. Steiner lectures on practical karma studies. On October 23, Annie Besant inducts Rudolf Steiner into the Esoteric School of the Theosophical Society. On October 25, Steiner begins a weekly series of lectures: 'The Field of Theosophy.' During this year, Rudolf Steiner also first meets Ita Wegman (1876–1943), who will become his close collaborator in his final years.

1903:   Rudolf Steiner holds about 300 lectures and seminars. In May, the first issue of the periodical *Luzifer* appears. In June, Rudolf Steiner visits London for the first meeting of the Federation of the European Sections of the Theosophical Society, where he meets Colonel Olcott. He begins to write *Theosophy* (CW 9).

1904:   Rudolf Steiner continues lecturing at the Workers' College and elsewhere (about 90 lectures), while lecturing intensively all over Germany among theosophists (about 140 lectures). In February, he meets Carl Unger (1878–1929), who will become a member of the board of the Anthroposophical Society (1913). In March, he meets Michael Bauer (1871–1929), a Christian mystic, who will also be on the board. In May, *Theosophy* appears, with the dedication: 'To the spirit of Giordano Bruno.' Rudolf Steiner and Marie von Sivers visit London for meetings with Annie Besant. June: Rudolf Steiner and Marie von Sivers attend the meeting of the Federation of European Sections of the Theosophical Society in Amsterdam. In July, Steiner begins the articles in *Luzifer-Gnosis* that will become *How to Know Higher Worlds* (CW 10) and *Cosmic Memory* (CW 11). In September, Annie Besant visits Germany. In December, Steiner lectures on Freemasonry. He mentions the High Grade Masonry derived from John Yarker and represented by Theodore Reuss and Karl Kellner as a blank slate 'into which a good image could be placed'.

1905:   This year, Steiner ends his non-theosophical lecturing activity. Supported by Marie von Sivers, his theosophical lecturing—both in public and in the Theosophical Society—increases significantly: 'The German Theosophical Movement is of exceptional importance.' Steiner recommends reading, among others, Fichte, Jacob Boehme, and Angelus Silesius. He begins to introduce Christian themes into Theosophy. He also begins to work with doctors (Felix Peipers and Ludwig Noll). In July, he is in London for the Federation of European Sections, where he attends a lecture by Annie Besant: 'I have seldom seen Mrs. Besant speak in so inward and heartfelt a manner... Through Mrs. Besant I have found the way to H.P. Blavatsky.' September to October, he gives a course of 31 lectures for a small group of esoteric students. In October, the annual meeting of the German Section of the Theosophical Society, which still remains very small, takes place. Rudolf Steiner reports membership has risen from 121 to 377 members. In November, seeking to establish esoteric 'continuity,' Rudolf Steiner and Marie von Sivers participate in a 'Memphis-Misraim' Masonic ceremony. They pay 45 marks for membership. 'Yesterday, you saw how little remains of former esoteric institutions.' 'We are dealing only with a "framework" . . for the present, nothing lies behind it. The occult powers have completely withdrawn.'

1906:   Expansion of theosophical work. Rudolf Steiner gives about 245 lectures, only 44 of which take place in Berlin. Cycles are given in Paris, Leipzig, Stuttgart, and Munich. Esoteric work also intensifies. Rudolf Steiner begins writing *An Outline of Esoteric Science* (CW 13). In January, Rudolf Steiner receives permission (a patent) from the Great Orient of the Scottish A & A Thirty-Three Degree Rite of the Order of the Ancient Freemasons of the Memphis-Misraim Rite to direct a chapter under the name 'Mystica Aeterna.' This will become the 'Cognitive-Ritual Section' (also called 'Misraim Service') of the Esoteric School. (See: *Freemasonry and Ritual Work: The Misraim Service,* CW 265.) During this time, Steiner also meets Albert Schweitzer. In May, he is in Paris, where he visits Édouard Schuré. Many Russians attend his lectures (including Konstantin Balmont, Dimitri Mereszkovski, Zinaida Hippius, and Maximilian Woloshin). He attends the General Meeting of the European Federation of the Theosophical Society, at which Col. Olcott is present for the last time. He spends the year's end in Venice and Rome, where he writes and works on his translation of H.P. Blavatsky's *Key to Theosophy.*

1907:   Further expansion of the German Theosophical Movement according to the Rosicrucian directive to 'introduce spirit into the world'—in education, in social questions, in art, and in science. In February, Col. Olcott dies in Adyar. Before he dies, Olcott indicates that 'the Masters' wish Annie Besant to succeed him: much politicking ensues. Rudolf Steiner supports Besant's candidacy. April–May: preparations for the Congress of the Federation of European Sections of the Theosophical Society—the great, watershed Whitsun 'Munich Congress,' attended by Annie Besant and others. Steiner decides to separate Eastern and Western (Christian–Rosicrucian) esoteric schools. He takes his esoteric school out of the Theosophical Society (Besant and Rudolf Steiner are 'in harmony' on this). Steiner makes his first lecture tours to Austria and Hungary. That summer, he is in Italy. In September, he visits Édouard Schuré, who will write the Introduction to the French edition of *Christianity as Mystical Fact* in Barr, Alsace. Rudolf Steiner writes the autobiographical statement known as the 'Barr Document.' In *Luzifer-Gnosis*, 'The Education of the Child' appears.

1908: The movement grows (membership: 1,150). Lecturing expands. Steiner makes his first extended lecture tour to Holland and Scandinavia, as well as visits to Naples and Sicily. Themes: St. John's Gospel, the Apocalypse, Egypt, science, philosophy, and logic. *Luzifer-Gnosis* ceases publication. In Berlin, Marie von Sivers (with Johanna Mücke (1864–1949) forms the *Philosophisch-Theosophisch* (after 1915 *Philosophisch-Anthroposophisch) Verlag* to publish Steiner's work. Steiner gives lecture cycles titled *The Gospel of St. John* (CW 103) and *The Apocalypse* (104).

1909: *An Outline of Esoteric Science* appears. Lecturing and travel continues. Rudolf Steiner's spiritual research expands to include the polarity of Lucifer and Ahriman; the work of great individualities in history; the Maitreya Buddha and the Bodhisattvas; spiritual economy (CW 109); the work of the spiritual hierarchies in heaven and on earth (CW 110). He also deepens and intensifies his research into the Gospels, giving lectures on the Gospel of St. Luke (CW 114) with the first mention of two Jesus children. Meets and becomes friends with Christian Morgenstern (1871–1914). In April, he lays the foundation stone for the Malsch model—the building that will lead to the first Goetheanum. In May, the International Congress of the Federation of European Sections of the Theosophical Society takes place in Budapest. Rudolf Steiner receives the Subba Row medal for *How to Know Higher Worlds*. During this time, Charles W. Leadbeater discovers Jiddu Krishnamurti (1895–1986) and proclaims him the future 'world teacher,' the bearer of the Maitreya Buddha and the 'reappearing Christ.' In October, Steiner delivers seminal lectures on 'anthroposophy,' which he will try, unsuccessfully, to rework over the next years into the unfinished work, *Anthroposophy (A Fragment)* (CW 45).

1910: New themes: *The Reappearance of Christ in the Etheric* (CW 118); *The Fifth Gospel; The Mission of Folk Souls* (CW 121); *Occult History* (CW 126); the evolving development of etheric cognitive capacities. Rudolf Steiner continues his Gospel research with *The Gospel of St. Matthew* (CW 123). In January, his father dies. In April, he takes a month-long trip to Italy, including Rome, Monte Cassino, and Sicily. He also visits Scandinavia again. July–August, he writes the first mystery drama, *The Portal of Initiation* (CW 14). In November, he gives 'psychosophy' lectures. In December, he submits 'On the

1911:

Psychological Foundations and Epistemological Framework of Theosophy' to the International Philosophical Congress in Bologna. The crisis in the Theosophical Society deepens. In January, 'The Order of the Rising Sun,' which will soon become 'The Order of the Star in the East,' is founded for the coming world teacher, Krishnamurti. At the same time, Marie von Sivers, Rudolf Steiner's co-worker, falls ill. Fewer lectures are given, but important new ground is broken. In Prague, in March, Steiner meets Franz Kafka (1883–1924) and Hugo Bergmann (1883–1975). In April, he delivers his paper to the Philosophical Congress. He writes the second mystery drama, *The Soul's Probation* (CW 14). Also, while Marie von Sivers is convalescing, Rudolf Steiner begins work on *Calendar 1912/1913*, which will contain the 'Calendar of the Soul' meditations. On March 19, Anna (Eunike) Steiner dies. In September, Rudolf Steiner visits Einsiedeln, birthplace of Paracelsus. In December, Friedrich Rittelmeyer, future founder of the Christian Community, meets Rudolf Steiner. The *Johannes-Bauverein,* the 'building committee,' which would lead to the first Goetheanum (first planned for Munich), is also founded, and a preliminary committee for the founding of an independent association is created that, in the following year, will become the Anthroposophical Society. Important lecture cycles include *Occult Physiology* (CW 128); *Wonders of the World* (CW 129); *From Jesus to Christ* (CW 131). Other themes: esoteric Christianity; Christian Rosenkreutz; the spiritual guidance of humanity; the sense world and the world of the spirit.

1912:

Despite the ongoing, now increasing crisis in the Theosophical Society, much is accomplished: *Calendar 1912/1913* is published; eurythmy is created; both the third mystery drama, *The Guardian of the Threshold* (CW 14) and *A Way of Self-Knowledge* (CW 16) are written. New (or renewed) themes included life between death and rebirth and karma and reincarnation. Other lecture cycles: *Spiritual Beings in the Heavenly Bodies and in the Kingdoms of Nature* (CW 136); *The Human Being in the Light of Occultism, Theosophy, and Philosophy* (CW 137); *The Gospel of St. Mark* (CW 139); and *The Bhagavad Gita and the Epistles of Paul* (CW 142). On May 8, Rudolf Steiner celebrates White Lotus Day, H.P. Blavatsky's death day, which he had faithfully observed for the past decade, for the last time. In August, Rudolf Steiner suggests the 'independent association' be called the 'Anthroposophical Society.' In September, the first eurythmy course takes place. In October, Rudolf Steiner declines recognition of a Theosophical Society lodge dedicated to the Star of the East and decides to expel all Theosophical Society members belonging to the order.

Also, with Marie von Sivers, he first visits Dornach, near Basel, Switzerland, and they stand on the hill where the Goetheanum will be built. In November, a Theosophical Society lodge is opened by direct mandate from Adyar (Annie Besant). In December, a meeting of the German section occurs at which it is decided that belonging to the Order of the Star of the East is incompatible with membership in the Theosophical Society. December 28: informal founding of the Anthroposophical Society in Berlin.

1913: Expulsion of the German section from the Theosophical Society. February 2–3: Foundation meeting of the Anthroposophical Society. Board members include: Marie von Sivers, Michael Bauer, and Carl Unger. September 20: Laying of the foundation stone for the *Johannes Bau* (Goetheanum) in Dornach. Building begins immediately. The third mystery drama, *The Soul's Awakening* (CW 14), is completed. Also: *The Threshold of the Spiritual World* (CW 147). Lecture cycles include: *The Bhagavad Gita and the Epistles of Paul* and *The Esoteric Meaning of the Bhagavad Gita* (CW 146), which the Russian philosopher Nikolai Berdyaev attends; *The Mysteries of the East and of Christianity* (CW 144); *The Effects of Esoteric Development* (CW 145); and *The Fifth Gospel* (CW 148). In May, Rudolf Steiner is in London and Paris, where anthroposophical work continues.

1914: Building continues on the *Johannes Bau* (Goetheanum) in Dornach, with artists and co-workers from seventeen nations. The general assembly of the Anthroposophical Society takes place. In May, Rudolf Steiner visits Paris, as well as Chartres Cathedral. June 28: assassination in Sarajevo ('Now the catastrophe has happened!'). August 1: War is declared. Rudolf Steiner returns to Germany from Dornach—he will travel back and forth. He writes the last chapter of *The Riddles of Philosophy*. Lecture cycles include: *Human and Cosmic Thought* (CW 151); *Inner Being of Humanity between Death and a New Birth* (CW 153); *Occult Reading and Occult Hearing* (CW 156). December 24: marriage of Rudolf Steiner and Marie von Sivers.

1915: Building continues. Life after death becomes a major theme, also art. Writes: *Thoughts during a Time of War* (CW 24). Lectures include: *The Secret of Death* (CW 159); *The Uniting of Humanity through the Christ Impulse* (CW 165).

1916: Rudolf Steiner begins work with Edith Maryon (1872–1924) on the sculpture 'The Representative of Humanity' ('The Group'— Christ, Lucifer, and Ahriman). He also works with the alchemist Alexander von Bernus on the quarterly *Das Reich*. He writes *The Riddle of Humanity* (CW 20). Lectures include: *Necessity and Freedom in World History and Human Action* (CW 166); *Past and Present in the*

Human Spirit (CW 167); *The Karma of Vocation* (CW 172); *The Karma of Untruthfulness* (CW 173).

1917: Russian Revolution. The U.S. enters the war. Building continues. Rudolf Steiner delineates the idea of the 'threefold nature of the human being' (in a public lecture March 15) and the 'threefold nature of the social organism' (hammered out in May–June with the help of Otto von Lerchenfeld and Ludwig Polzer-Hoditz in the form of two documents titled *Memoranda,* which were distributed in high places). August–September: Rudolf Steiner writes *The Riddles of the Soul* (CW 20). Also: commentary on 'The Chymical Wedding of Christian Rosenkreutz' for Alexander Bernus (Das *Reich*). Lectures include: *The Karma of Materialism* (CW 176); *The Spiritual Background of the Outer World: The Fall of the Spirits of Darkness* (CW 177).

1918: March 18: peace treaty of Brest-Litovsk—'Now everything will truly enter chaos! What is needed is cultural renewal.' June: Rudolf Steiner visits Karlstein (Grail) Castle outside Prague. Lecture cycle: *From Symptom to Reality in Modern History* (CW 185). In mid-November, Emil Molt, of the Waldorf-Astoria Cigarette Company, has the idea of founding a school for his workers' children.

1919: Focus on the threefold social organism: tireless travel, countless lectures, meetings, and publications. At the same time, a new public stage of Anthroposophy emerges as cultural renewal begins. The coming years will see initiatives in pedagogy, medicine, pharmacology, and agriculture. January 27: threefold meeting: 'We must first of all, with the money we have, found free schools that can bring people what they need.' February: first public eurythmy performance in Zurich. Also: 'Appeal to the German People' (CW 24), circulated March 6 as a newspaper insert. In April, *Towards Social Renewal* (CW 23) appears—'perhaps the most widely read of all books on politics appearing since the war'. Rudolf Steiner is asked to undertake the 'direction and leadership' of the school founded by the Waldorf-Astoria Company. Rudolf Steiner begins to talk about the 'renewal' of education. May 30: a building is selected and purchased for the future Waldorf School. August–September, Rudolf Steiner gives a lecture course for Waldorf teachers, *The Foundations of Human Experience (Study of Man)* (CW 293). September 7: Opening of the first Waldorf School. December (into January): first science course, the *Light Course* (CW 320).

1920: The Waldorf School flourishes. New threefold initiatives. Founding of limited companies *Der Kommende Tag* and *Futurum A.G.* to infuse spiritual values into the economic realm. Rudolf Steiner also focuses on the sciences. Lectures: *Introducing Anthroposophical*

Medicine (CW 312); *The Warmth Course* (CW 321); *The Boundaries of Natural Science* (CW 322); *The Redemption of Thinking* (CW 74). February: Johannes Werner Klein—later a co-founder of the Christian Community—asks Rudolf Steiner about the possibility of a 'religious renewal,' a 'Johannine church.' In March, Rudolf Steiner gives the first course for doctors and medical students. In April, a divinity student asks Rudolf Steiner a second time about the possibility of religious renewal. September 27–October 16: anthroposophical 'university course.' December: lectures titled *The Search for the New Isis* (CW 202).

1921:   Rudolf Steiner continues his intensive work on cultural renewal, including the uphill battle for the threefold social order. 'University' arts, scientific, theological, and medical courses include: *The Astronomy Course* (CW 323); *Observation, Mathematics, and Scientific Experiment* (CW 324); the *Second Medical Course* (CW 313); *Colour*. In June and September–October, Rudolf Steiner also gives the first two 'priests' courses' (CW 342 and 343). The 'youth movement' gains momentum. Magazines are founded: *Die Drei* (January), and—under the editorship of Albert Steffen (1884–1963)—the weekly, *Das Goetheanum* (August). In February–March, Rudolf Steiner takes his first trip outside Germany since the war (Holland). On April 7, Steiner receives a letter regarding 'religious renewal,' and May 22–23, he agrees to address the question in a practical way. In June, the Klinical-Therapeutic Institute opens in Arlesheim under the direction of Dr. Ita Wegman. In August, the Chemical-Pharmaceutical Laboratory opens in Arlesheim (Oskar Schmiedel and Ita Wegman are directors). The Clinical Therapeutic Institute is inaugurated in Stuttgart (Dr. Ludwig Noll is director); also the Research Laboratory in Dornach (Ehrenfried Pfeiffer and Gunther Wachsmuth are directors). In November–December, Rudolf Steiner visits Norway.

1922:   The first half of the year involves very active public lecturing (thousands attend); in the second half, Rudolf Steiner begins to withdraw and turn toward the Society—'The Society is asleep.' It is 'too weak' to do what is asked of it. The businesses—*Der Kommende Tag* and *Futurum A.G.*—fail. In January, with the help of an agent, Steiner undertakes a twelve-city German lecture tour, accompanied by eurythmy performances. In two weeks he speaks to more than 2,000 people. In April, he gives a 'university course' in The Hague. He also visits England. In June, he is in Vienna for the East–West Congress. In August–September, he is back in England for the Oxford Conference on Education. Returning to Dornach, he gives the lectures *Philosophy, Cosmology, and Religion*

(CW 215), and gives the third priests' course (CW 344). On September 16, The Christian Community is founded. In October–November, Steiner is in Holland and England. He also speaks to the youth: *The Youth Course* (CW 217). In December, Steiner gives lectures titled *The Origins of Natural Science* (CW 326), and *Humanity and the World of Stars: The Spiritual Communion of Humanity* (CW 219). December 31: Fire at the Goetheanum, which is destroyed.

1923:   Despite the fire, Rudolf Steiner continues his work unabated. A very hard year. Internal dispersion, dissension, and apathy abound. There is conflict—between old and new visions—within the Society. A wake-up call is needed, and Rudolf Steiner responds with renewed lecturing vitality. His focus: the spiritual context of human life; initiation science; the course of the year; and community building. As a foundation for an artistic school, he creates a series of pastel sketches. Lecture cycles: *The Anthroposophical Movement; Initiation Science* (CW 227) (in Wales at the Penmaenmawr Summer School); *The Four Seasons and the Archangels* (CW 229); *Harmony of the Creative Word* (CW 230); *The Supersensible Human* (CW 231), given in Holland for the founding of the Dutch society. On November 10, in response to the failed Hitler-Ludendorff putsch in Munich, Steiner closes his Berlin residence and moves the *Philosophisch-Anthroposophisch Verlag* (Press) to Dornach. On December 9, Steiner begins the serialization of his *Autobiography: The Course of My Life* (CW 28) in *Das Goetheanum*. It will continue to appear weekly, without a break, until his death. Late December–early January: Rudolf Steiner re-founds the Anthroposophical Society (about 12,000 members internationally) and takes over its leadership. The new board members are: Marie Steiner, Ita Wegman, Albert Steffen, Elisabeth Vreede, and Gunther Wachsmuth. (See *The Christmas Meeting for the Founding of the General Anthroposophical Society,* CW 260.) Accompanying lectures: *Mystery Knowledge and Mystery Centres* (CW 232); *World History in the Light of Anthroposophy* (CW 233). December 25: the Foundation Stone is laid (in the hearts of members) in the form of the 'Foundation Stone Meditation.'

1924:   January 1: having founded the Anthroposophical Society and taken over its leadership, Rudolf Steiner has the task of 'reforming' it. The process begins with a weekly newssheet ('What's Happening in the Anthroposophical Society') in which Rudolf Steiner's 'Letters to Members' and 'Anthroposophical Leading Thoughts' appear (CW 26). The next step is the creation of a new esoteric class, the 'first class' of the 'University of Spiritual Science' (which was to have been followed, had Rudolf Steiner lived longer, by two more advanced classes). Then comes a new language for

Anthroposophy—practical, phenomenological, and direct; and Rudolf Steiner creates the model for the second Goetheanum. He begins the series of extensive 'karma' lectures (CW 235–40); and finally, responding to needs, he creates two new initiatives: biodynamic agriculture and curative education. After the middle of the year, rumours begin to circulate regarding Steiner's health. Lectures: January–February, *Anthroposophy* (CW 234); February: *Tone Eurythmy* (CW 278); June: *The Agriculture Course* (CW 327); June–July: *Speech Eurythmy* (CW 279); *Curative Education* (CW 317); August: (England, 'Second International Summer School'), *Initiation Consciousness: True and False Paths in Spiritual Investigation* (CW 243); September: *Pastoral Medicine* (CW 318). On September 26, for the first time, Rudolf Steiner cancels a lecture. On September 28, he gives his last lecture. On September 29, he withdraws to his studio in the carpenter's shop; now he is definitively ill. Cared for by Ita Wegman, he continues working, however, and writing the weekly installments of his *Autobiography* and *Letters to the Members/ Leading Thoughts* (CW 26).

1925:   Rudolf Steiner, while continuing to work, continues to weaken. He finishes *Extending Practical Medicine* (CW 27) with Ita Wegman. On March 30, around ten in the morning, Rudolf Steiner dies.

INDEX

Steiner

A NOTE FROM RUDOLF STEINER PRESS

We are an independent publisher and registered charity (non-profit organisation) dedicated to making available the work of Rudolf Steiner in English translation. We care a great deal about the content of our books and have hundreds of titles available – as printed books, ebooks and in audio formats.

As a publisher devoted to anthroposophy...

- We continually commission translations of previously unpublished works by Rudolf Steiner and invest in re-translating, editing and improving our editions.

- We are committed to making anthroposophy available to all by publishing introductory books as well as contemporary research.

- Our new print editions and ebooks are carefully checked and proofread for accuracy, and converted into all formats for all platforms.

- Our translations are officially authorised by Rudolf Steiner's estate in Dornach, Switzerland, to whom we pay royalties on sales, thus assisting their critical work.

So, look out for Rudolf Steiner Press as a mark of quality and support us today by buying our books, or contact us should you wish to sponsor specific titles or to support the charity with a gift or legacy.

office@rudolfsteinerpress.com
Join our e-mailing list at www.rudolfsteinerpress.com

RUDOLF STEINER PRESS